ROMANOV FAMILY YEARBOOK:
On This Date in Their Own Words

HELEN AZAR

with Amanda Madru

ACKNOWLEDGMENTS

Many thanks to staff of State Archives of Russian Federation (GARF) for their assistance; Aleksandar Tanasijevic, Alena Dufkova and Igor Sikorsky Jr for the images. And of course, thank you, the readers and fellow Russian imperial history enthusiasts, for allowing the members of the last Russian imperial family speak through your continuing interest and support!

The Romanov Family Yearbook

Dramatis Personae:

- Emperor Nicholas II Alexandrovich of Russia (1868-1918)
- Empress Alexandra Feodorovna, nee Princess Alix of Hesse (1872-1918)
- Grand Duchess Olga Nikolaevna - eldest daughter of Nicholas and Alexandra (1895-1918)
- Grand Duchess Tatiana Nikolaevna - second daughter of Nicholas and Alexandra (1897-1918)
- Grand Duchess Maria Nikolaevna - third daughter of Nicholas and Alexandra (1899-1918)
- Grand Duchess Anastasia Nikolaevna - fourth daughter of Nicholas and Alexandra (190-1918)
- Tsesarevich Alexei Nikolaevich – youngest child and only son of Nicholas and Alexandra (1904-1918)
- Grand Duke Michael Alexandrovich – younger brother of Nicholas II (1878-1918)
- Grand Duke Dmitri Pavlovich – first cousin of Nicholas II (1891-1942)
- Anna Alexandrovna Vyrubova – lady-in-waiting and confidante to Empress Alexandra. Close friend of the Romanov family (1884-1964)

The story of the downfall of the Romanov Dynasty is well-known—following the Russian Revolution, members of imperial family and those closest to them, as well as other individuals known to harbor monarchist sympathies, were to be politically executed. They simply disappeared, never to be seen again. For the duration of the Soviet period, photographs and documents pertaining to the tsarist regime were kept under lock and key, and it was largely forbidden to so much as mention the Romanovs or what happened to them. After the fall of the Soviet Union in 1991, however, investigations began, and the remains of the last tsar, his immediate family (with the exception of his son and one of his daughters, whose remains would not be found until 2007), and the four loyal retainers who followed them through life and death, were rediscovered in the far reaches of Siberia, where their killers had been hoped that no one would ever trek.

This discovery would lead to a revival of interest in the family that once ruled the largest empire on earth, and slowly, many of their personal photographs, letters, and diaries—all carefully preserved—came to light. It has only been in recent years that author Helen Azar has released her original translations of these documents, making them accessible to those who do not speak Russian. Here, in her newest book of letters and diary entries ranging from 1904 to 1918—Azar gives new life to the last Romanovs. In addition to the words of Nicholas II, Empress Alexandra, and their five children, *The Romanov Family Yearbook* includes previously unpublished letters written by Nicholas II's younger brother, Grand Duke Michael Alexandrovich and his first cousin, Grand Duke Dmitri Pavlovich, as well as memories from close family friend Anna Alexandrovna Vyrubova.

Of those whose writings this book contains, only Grand Duke Dmitri and Anna Vyrubova would live to remember the Romanovs. Grand Duke Michael was killed in Perm on 13 June, 1918, and a little over a month later, his brother and sister-in-law, along with their five children and four faithful servants, would be herded into a small cellar in Ekaterinburg, where they would meet their ultimate brutal fate.

Summer of 2018 will mark a century since these untimely and tragic deaths. Through Azar's translations, these once-shadowy figures from the past will speak from beyond the grave, telling us not only of the extraordinary historical events to which they were both witnesses and key players, but of their surprisingly ordinary daily lives. *The Romanov Family Yearbook,* in commemoration of this centennial year, 2018, honors those who are gone by keeping their memory alive.

JANUARY

From the 1916 diary of Alexei Romanov:

January 1. Got up late today. Had tea at 10 o'clock, then went to [see] Mama. Mama is not feeling well, so she was lying down all day. Sat at home, because I have a cold. Had breakfast with Olga, Tatiana, Maria and Anastasia. In the afternoon went to Kolya's[1] and played there. It was really fun. Had dinner at 6

---

[1] Alexei's playmate Nikolai Vladimirovich Derevenko, son of family physician Dr. Vladimir Nikolaevich Derevenko.

o'clock, then played. At 8 o'cl. was at Mama's during their dinner. At 10 o'cl. was in bed.

January 2. Got up late. Did not take a walk. Read in English. Had breakfast with O., T., M., A. Mama stayed in bed. Did not walk during the day. Played with Alexei and Sergei. Had dinner at 6 o'clock. At 8 o'cl. was at dinner at Mama's. Went to bed late.

From 1917 diary of Olga Romanov:

Minevich. Tuesday. **3rd January**. We 2 to Znamenie[2] and to the infirmary[3]. Abashidze had surgery. Removed shrapnel from his neck. Made a lot of beds, changed dressings, set up, etc. There was enough to

---

[2] Church at Tsarskoe Selo.
[3] The two eldest grand duchesses received their nursing certificates at the start of the war, and worked at a military infirmary.

do. Fed Merkuriev. Voskanov and D[illegible] were transferred. Ate all together. We 4 went to the Grand Palace[4]—at about 4 o'clock we 3 took a walk with Papa. Very cold, 16 deg. of frost, bright in the evening. At 6 o'clock went to Anya's[5] and sat with the Cossacks. Aleks. K., Vikt. and Yuzik, like last time in front of the fireplace. After that, only one lamp was lit on the floor, [we] took turns sitting in the comfortable chair, fought with Vikt. [illegible] with pillows and pushed each other hard for the best chair. It was so cozy and nice. Alex.[ei]'s voice is somewhat better. Lishevich had dinner. [He] spoke nicely with Mama. Her voice is also hoarse. Papa read Chekhov to us, "The Teacher." After that [I] wrote to Anya's dictation the words and notes of Father Grigori. After 11o'clock to bed. Al. is [doing] fine, [he] took a walk.

---

[4] The Catherine Palace.
[5] Anna Alexandrovna Vyrubova, close friend of the imperial family.

From the 1913 diary of Olga Romanov:

Friday. **4 January**. We four rode with Trina.[6] Mama did not sleep well and is feeling poorly. Had breakfast with Papa and dear General Dumbadze.[7] At 2 o'cl. 7 min. Tatiana, Lili Obolenskaya[8]and I went to Grandmama's[9] in Petersburg. We stayed there for about an hour and then went to Aunt Olga's with Irina. Had tea there with her, Aunt Ksenia,[10] Aunt Minnie[11] and Madame Steckel with her daughter Zoya. Stayed there until 6 o'cl. It was lots of fun. After that

---

[6] Catherine Adolphovna Schneider, friend and Russian tutor of the empress.
[7] Ivan Antonovich Dumbadze, the tsar's major-general.
[8] Princess Elizaveta Obolenskaya, a maid of honor to the empress.
[9] Dowager Empress Maria Feodorovna, the tsar's mother.
[10] Grand Duchess Ksenia Alexandrovna, sister of the tsar.
[11] Grand Duchess Maria Georgievna, wife of Grand Duke Georgiy Mikhailovich.

Zoya, Irina[12] and I went to her [house]. Later returned with Olga Yevgenievna[13] at 7 o'cl. 15 min. Prayed with Alexei as usual. Had dinner and spent the evening with Papa and Mama. N.P.[14] left for Sevastopol tonight. May the Lord save him.

From the 1916 diary of Maria Romanov:

5 January. In the morning went to church with O[lga], T[atiana] and Al[exei]. Mama is in bed. In the afternoon walked around the city with T. and Isa.[15] Had tea with O., T. and Anya near Mama. Went to vsenoshnaya[16] with O., T. and Alexei. Had dinner 3 and Mama [was] on the sofa. Anastasia was in bed as

---

[12] Princess Irina Alexandrovna, daughter of Grand Duchess Ksenia Alexandrovna.
[13] Lady-in-waiting Olga Yevgenievna Butsova.
[14] Nikolai Pavlovich Sablin, the tsar's aide-de-camp.
[15] Baroness Sophia Karlovna von Buxhoeveden, lady-in-waiting to the empress.
[16] Evening prayer services, the all-night vigil.

she has a cold, she has high fever. Got a letter from Darling Papa.

From the 1916 diary of Alexei Romanov:

6 January. Got up late. At 11 o'clock in the morning went to the Palace infirmary. Had breakfast with O., T., M. Mama and Anastasia stayed in bed all day. Anastasia has bronchitis. During the day took a walk outside then went to Kolya's. Had dinner at 6 o'cl. Sat at Mama's after their dinner. To bed at half [past] 10 o'cl.

From the 1913 diary of Nicholas II:

7th January. Monday. Got up late, but had the chance to take a walk. After Grigorovich's report received two governors and Gen. Dobronravov. Minnie came for breakfast. Took a walk with the daughters. At 4 1/4 they had a Yolka [party] for the officers. Olga Alexandrovna came to [my] daughters' aid, who then had tea with us. From 6 o'cl. until 7 ½ received the first report from Maklakov. Godspeed to him! Grabbe[17] (on duty) had dinner. Read in the evening.

---

[17] Count Alexander Grabbe, aide-de-camp to the tsar

From the 1915 diary of Tatiana Romanov:

Thursday, **8 January**. Had a lesson in the morning. Two went to Znamenie from there to the infirmary. Bandaged Kusov, Veselovsky, Belitsky and Gordinsky. Went to the Big House for appendicitis [surgery]. Handled instruments. Breakfast with Papa, Uncle Boris[18] and Ioann.[19] Mama on the sofa. In the afternoon went with Mama to the infirmary. Went to [see] Anya. Then sat and worked at Nizhegorodtzy's. Had tea and dinner with Papa and Mama. Had lessons. At 9:16 Olga and I went back to the

---

[18] Grand Duke Boris Vladimirovich, the tsar's first cousin.
[19] Prince Ioann Konstantinovich, eldest son of Grand Duke Konstantin Konstantinovich.

infirmary. Cleaned the instruments in the dressing room for tomorrow with Nurse Grekova. [She was] awfully sweet. Then sat with Anya for a bit, later with Nizhegorodtzy. They were awfully sweet. Walked around to say goodbye to everyone.

From 1913 diary of Olga Romanov:

Wednesday. **9 January**. Had 2 history lessons: Russian History and World History. There was no German lesson. Did not have lessons in the afternoon, since we were supposed to go to Grandmama's for a Christmas Party, but did not go because Aunt Ksenia and Vasya[20] have the flu. Had breakfast with Papa. Mama got up only for tea. She is still not feeling well— her heart or her head. In the afternoon we 4 walked with Papa. The weather was wonderful: 13 degrees

---

[20] Prince Vasily Alexandrovich, son of Grand Duchess Ksenia Alexandrovna.

below, bright sun, sky and moon. Slid down the hill by the white tower.[21] Had tea with Papa and Mama. Before dinner T.[atiana] and I played the piano in four hands. After that prayed with Alexei. In the evening sat at Mama's. Papa read in his [room] and came over to Mama's [room] after 10 o'cl.[ock]. Anya and I helped her paste photographs into the album and knitted. Went to bed after 10 o'clock.

1917 letter from Tatiana to Nicholas II:

10 January. My dear Papa darling! I am writing to you now before obednya.[22] It is snowing mixed with

---

[21] A gothic-style pavilion in the park of the Alexander Palace.
[22] Holy liturgy.

rain because it is one degree of warmth, we have had this weather for three days already. We saw Nik. [olai] Pav. [lovich], he alone came over two or three times, and yesterday he left for Golsinforsk. One of these days N.N. Rodionov[23] is supposed to arrive, and I am very happy. We have not seen him for almost a year. Alexei and Anastasia are both moving their beds into the playroom, where they lie next to each other all day. During the day we all have tea up there. The [Christmas] tree still stands, so cozy. It will be sad to take it down, but for now it is not dropping its needles, so it is fine. So tiresome that Mama still does not feel well, but she still gets up during the day and lies on the sofa a little there. We take turns going to Anya's so that she doesn't get too bored lying in bed. The other day Emelyanov had surgery, remember him? He was at the Christmas party at the Arena. They removed a bullet fragment from his bone. Now he is in a lot of pain, but the rest are fine. Well, goodbye, Papa my darling dear. We have to go to church. May God bless you, I kiss You very very hard as I love you. Your faithful Voznesenetz.[24]

---

[23] Nikolai Nikolaevich Rodionov.
[24] Refers to the 8th Voznesensky Uhlan Regiment, of which Tatiana was honorary colonel.

Letter from Anastasia to Nicholas II:

11 January, 1916. Tsarskoe Selo. My dear Papa Darling! I am still in bed, but I think tomorrow I will get up for the first time. My bronchitis is gone now. In the morning before breakfast I stay in bed in my room and write or Shura[25] reads to me, and I go to the playroom for breakfast, and there get into bed. Mama comes for tea and sits until 6 o'cl. Yesterday Alexei was in a very military mood, what he did not do, he was so terribly funny. Now we have nice weather, the sun comes out and not much melts, so that it is rather warm and nice. Tomorrow is a month since the 1st Hundred left Mogilev.[26] Yesterday we all wrote to Aunt Olga,[27] as some man was going there. It's such a

---

[25] Alexandra Alexandrovna Tegleva, nurse to the imperial children and eventual wife of Pierre Gilliard.
[26] City where military headquarters were located.
[27] Grand Duchess Olga Alexandrovna, younger sister of the tsar.

shame that they took your little shovel, but hope that they gave you a new one, or the same one! Mordvinov[28] is probably charming, yes? We will soon have breakfast with Alexei, but he will not finish very fast, while I am done in 10 min. or faster. Mama will now sit on the balcony with Maria. "Ortipo"[29] and "Joy"[30] asked to send [you] big regards and to tell you that they miss you. I am so bored sitting in bed and being unable to go to our infirmary—this is desperately boring. I send you awfully big 1000 kisses. May God keep you. Your loving loyal and faithful Kaspiyitz.

---

[28] Colonel Anatoly Alexandrovich Mordvinov, of His Majesty's Own Life-Guards Cuirassiers Regiment.
[29] Tatiana's pet dog.
[30] Alexei's pet dog.

From the 1913 diary of Tatiana Romanov:

12th January, Saturday. [Tatiana's Name Day – N.S. 25 January] In the morning went to Mama's and received a lot of nice gifts. Moleben[31] at 12 1/2. Before that went to Mama's for a little while and then sat upstairs, responded to telegrams. Aunt Olga arrived and we four went with her to moleben here at home. Had breakfast four with Papa, Aunt Olga and Sashka [Vorontsov]. In the afternoon everyone went to our ice rink, and slid down the ice hill. Then Sashka came over. It was such fun to slide with them. At 4 o'clock [we] returned home and Irina came over. Had

---

[31] Intercessory prayer service

tea with them downstairs. Aunt Olga left and we went to the regimental church.[32] Had dinner four with Papa, Irina, Anya and Sashka. I sat between them, I mean [between] Anya and Sashka. Later [we] went to have coffee in the big room for a little while. Then Sashka left and we went to Mama's. I started pasting Anya's photographs. At 10 ½ went to bed.

From the 1917 diary of Olga Romanov:

Count Zamoisky. Thursday. **12th January**. We 2 to the infirmary. Wrote, distributed medicine and made up beds on the 2nd ward with Nurse Shevchuk. Volga is leaving. Changed dressings on Abashev's neck, etc. Volodya,[33] Motzidarsky, Fedya Baroshkov, Lieutenant

---

[32] Cathedral at Tsarskoe Selo
[33] Vladimir Kiknadze, one of Tatiana's favorite soldiers

[illegible] came by to congratulate T.[atiana]. At 12 ½ [they] left. D[illegible] [was] at the church for prayers. Uncle Mimi[34] had breakfast. M.[aria] and I walked with Papa. Around 5 deg. frost, nice, quiet. After tea 6 o'clock cinematograph. "Tayinstvenaya ruka", etc. Mama wasn't there. In the evening Papa, as usual, read after 10 o'clock, Chekh[ov]'s "Myslitel", "Doch Albiona", "Na Chuzhbine", "Kuharka Zhenit'sya" and "Drama." After 11 o'clock to bed.

From the 1913 diary of Nicholas II:

13th January. Monday. Took a nice walk in the morning; the weather was sad, it was raining. After

---

[34] Grand Duke Mikhail Alexandrovich

Grigorovich's report, received until breakfast. Around 3 o'cl. Alexei was presented with zemstvos[35] at the Grand Palace—a village made by craftsmen on an extremely long table. After that took a walk with Olga and Marie; the rest have a cold. Was finally free, i.e. was able to study peacefully.

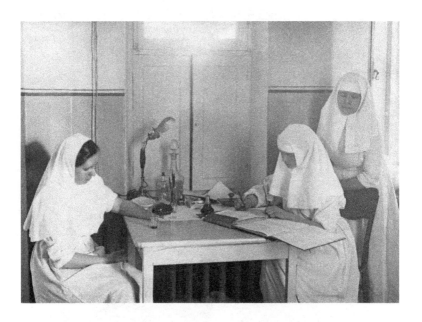

From the 1917 diary of Olga Romanov:

Stefanovich. Saturday, **14th January**. Zborovosky. We 2 to Znamenie and to the infirmary. Rita[36] got Ward II for Volga, her substitute is S. Freidlikh, while Alice— [substitutes for] Olga Porf. Mikhalsky had surgery, [they] removed shrapnel from his shoulder.

---

[35] Gifted land
[36] Margarita Sergeyevna Khitrovo, lady-in-waiting and friend of Olga Nikolaevna

Everything is fine. Wrote, distributed medicine, etc. as always. Count Fredericks had breakfast. M.[aria] and I walked with Papa. 4 deg. [of] frost. It is snowing. Lyolya Makarov came to see Al.[exei] before breakfast. We 4 and Papa [went] to vsenoshnaya. Stefanovich had dinner. In the evening Papa read "Captain's Uniform" and "Living Chronology" to us.

From the 1916 diary of Alexei Romanov:

15 January. Got up at ½ 9. In the morning studied French and God's Law. Did not take a walk. Had breakfast with O., T., M. and A. Mama was lying down all day. During the day [I] played with [toy] soldiers. Had tea at Mama's. Had dinner at 6 o'cl. Dinner was at Mama's. Went to bed early.

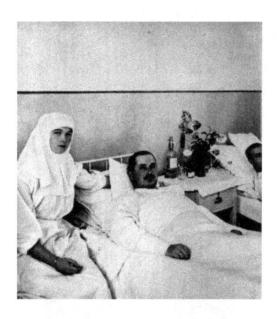

From the 1917 diary of Olga Romanov:

Vilkitsky. Monday. **16th January**. To Znamenie and to the infirmary, we 2. Did the same as always, made the beds, wrote, fed Pop[ov], etc. Zaremba tried to walk with the help of his 2 nurses. Vilkitsky had breakfast. At 3 o'clock M.[aria] and I walked with Papa. As always, the sun came out. Papa is in a good mood, Mama still tired— [we] did nothing unusual. Vilkitsky had dinner. After 10 ¼ Papa came over and read "The Exclamation Point," "Well, Public," "He Over-salted," "He Poured" and "Chameleon."

From the 1916 diary of Alexei Romanov:

17 January. Got up early. Went to obednya. Then [we] rode to the station at 12 o'cl. to meet Papa. Had breakfast with Papa, Mama, O., T., M., A. Then rested and took a walk. Then had tea. Had dinner at 6 o'cl. Was at dinner at Papa's. Later [I] played. Went to bed early.

18 January. Got up early. Studied and took a walk. Had breakfast 5, Papa and Mama. Took a walk during the day by the W[hite] Tower. Then studied and did homework. Went to tea at Mama's. Had dinner at 6 o'cl. At 8 o'cl. went to obednya. Went to bed late.

From the 1904 diary of Nicholas II:

19ᵗʰ January. Monday. The morning was very busy and in general a very tiring day. Received reports and all sorts of representatives from 4 o'cl. The walk refreshed my mind. Studied until 7 o'cl. Andrei (on duty) had dinner. At 9 ½ the **big ball** began. There were more people there than ever. There were enough seats for all at supper. Went around the tables in all the halls. Luckily dear Alix withstood the ball excellently. Having returned to [my] rooms at 1 ¼ and undressed, [we] had a light snack here as usual.

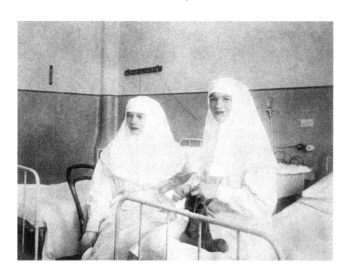

From the 1917 diary of Olga Romanov:

N.P. Sablin.[37] Friday. **20th January**. Directly to the infirmary, there were a lot of dressings [to do]. Wrote [notes] on both wards, distributed medicines, made the beds, etc. Fed Kamenetsky. [...]. Had not seen him for 2 years. The British millionaires had breakfast, N.P. and Valya Dolgorukov.[38] During the day walked with Papa, we 2 and Shvybz.[39] Sunny, very cold. 18 of frost. After tea cinematograph at Al.'s. In the evening 37.7°. N.P. had dinner. Nothing unusual happened in the evening. Mama is more or less fine. At 11 o'clock to bed.

---

[37] Nikolai Pavlovich Sablin, the tsar's aide-de-camp.
[38] Prince Vasily Alexandrovich Dolgorukov.
[39] One of Anastasia's nicknames.

Mordvinov. Saturday. **21st Jan**.

Kolesnikov. Directly to the infirmary, we 2. Kasyanov
finally returned. Distributed medicines, made the
beds, set up some [patients], and wrote. Nikolaev did
not feel well, then it passed. [I] changed the dressings
on Ponomarev's hand. Mordvinov and Count
Fredericks had breakfast. [It is] sunny and very cold.
In the morning 25 of frost. Stayed home. With Mama
saw two Englishwomen, Sybil Grey and another one.
Then [saw] Anya, Alya and Seryozha. Had tea, as
always and then cinematograph at Al.[exei]'s. About 7
o'clock, we 4 with Mama to vsenoshnaya. Papa
received. He had dinner with a mass of foreigners,
while we [ate] with Mama. She plans on receiving
Strashikh just now. He came after 10 o'clock. Early
to bed.

Thursday, **22 January**. At 9.30 [we] 4 went with Papa
and Mama to church for moleben. At 10 o'clock Papa
departed. So sad. [We] two went to the infirmary.
Bandaged Krat, Gordinsky, Belitsky, Otmarshteyn and
Gumanyuk. Took photographs in each ward.
Breakfast and lunch with Mama. At 2 o'clock
Gogoberidze came to say goodbye at Mama's. Then
[we] walked. Sat a little with Alexei, who is in bed as
[his] leg and arm ache. Went to the Grand Palace.
Had tea with Mama upstairs at Alexei's. Had lessons.
After lunch we went to [see] ours. Sat with the
Nizhegorodtzy. Put together a puzzle with Navruzov
and Vachnadze, then worked. Returned, sat with
Mama.

From the 1915 diary of Tatiana Romanov:

Thursday, **22 January**. At 9.30 [we] 4 went with Papa
and Mama to church for moleben. At 10 o'clock Papa
departed. So sad. [We] two went to the infirmary.
Bandaged Krat, Gordinsky, Belitsky, Otmarshteyn and
Gumanyuk. Took photographs in each ward.
Breakfast and lunch with Mama. At 2 o'clock
Gogoberidze came to say goodbye at Mama's. Then
[we] walked. Sat a little with Alexei, who is in bed as
[his] leg and arm ache. Went to the Grand Palace.
Had tea with Mama upstairs at Alexei's. Had lessons.
After lunch we went to [see] ours. Sat with the
Nizhcgorodtzy. Put together a puzzle with Navruzov
and Vachnadze, then worked. Returned, sat with
Mama.

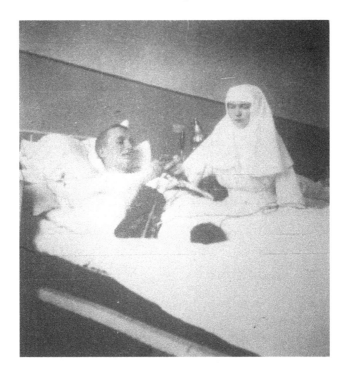

From the 1917 diary of Olga Romanov:

Prince Ernstov. Monday. **23rd January**. Directly to the infirmary. Wrote a lot, arranged flowers, then the medicines. Fed Pop[ov]. Everyone is fine. The little nurse, Kotenovskaya was there. Prince Ernestov and Prince Kastelno, [and] the French had breakfast. At 2 ½ at [illegible]. Papa was receiving [illegible] 200 officers who graduated from the higher military academy. Mama gave out the [holy] images. We just stood there. It lasted two hours and of course they were tired. Papa [is] "plastun."[40]   After tea

---

[40] Infantry Cossack regiment.

cinematograph at Al.'s. 20 [degrees] of frost. Sunny. [I] did the pulverization of Shareiko's throat. Prince Ernestov and Anya had dinner. In the evening Papa read an interesting report from the commander of the battleship "Chezma" and the report from Captain Tr. Schultz of the English Navy. After that, Chekhov's "Anyuta." "In Moscow on Trubnaya Plaza" and "Horse Family Name." Count Sheremetiev.[41]

Tuesday. **24th January.** Directly to the infirmary. Not much to do—wrote, fixed the beds, etc. Talked to Kasyanov. He played 2 new things on the piano and sang along. He is signing up for ambulatory treatment, like Biserov. Carol of Romania[42] had breakfast. At 3 [I] went for a walk with Papa. 12-13 [degrees] of frost. Walked around the garden. After tea cinematograph at Al.[exei]'s. T.[atiana] and I had [our] hair washed and curled. In the evening [did] nothing unusual. Papa wrote in his album. At 11 o'clock to bed as usual.

---

[41] Count Alexander Sheremetiev.
[42] Prince Carol of Romania.

From the 1916 diary of Alexei Romanov:

24 January. Got up early. Took a walk. Had breakfast with Mama. Took a walk in the afternoon. At 5 o'cl. went to tea at Mama's, where Rodionov was [too]. At 6 o'cl. ate dinner. At 8 o'cl. was at to dinner at Mama's. Went to bed late.

1915 letter from Anastasia to Nicholas II:

25 January. My precious Papa darling! Now we are going to church. The weather is wonderful now, the sun shines so nicely. Yesterday Mama's train arrived with the wounded. I wish I were with you! I will finish this letter later as I will be late for church. Well, we just got back from our infirmary. 11 lower ranks arrived there. This one poor young officer, who was injured in the head and therefore cannot speak and can barely hear. I got a letter from a soldier. We went to Glindeman's wedding, he is from the 3rd Sharpshooter regiment. His current wife is sweet and very young. Their wedding took place at the Palace lower church. Of course, there was some confusion prior to it, because no one knew where it will take place, and poor Glindeman ran around and did not know what to do. Right now, we will have tea, but Mama and Olga and Tatiana have not returned from the Grand Palace yet. They have been there for over an hour already. Regards to Nikolai Pavlovich and to Mordvinov too. Vachnadze can walk already, he is a Nizhegorodetz.[43] Well, I think I told you everything we did. Kiss to Aunt Olga. Goodbye, Papa darling. I give you a big kiss, your loving daughter Nastasia

---

[43] From Nizhny Novgorod.

Shvybzik. ANRPKZSG.[44] May the Lord be with you!
Sleep well and see me in your dreams.

From the 1916 diary of Alexei Romanov:

26 January. Got up early. In the morning studied,
then took a walk. Had breakfast with Papa, Mama
and we 5. Three days ago, a rabid dog bit Joy and
Brom in Bablovsk. Took a walk during the day. At 5
o'cl. was at tea at Mama's. Had dinner at 6 o'cl. with
V. Nikolaevich [Derevenko].[45] At 8 o'cl. was at Mama's
for dinner. Went to bed late. In the evening Grigori
was here.

---

[44] Some of Anastasia's nicknames.
[45] Dr. Vladimir Nikolaevich Derevenko.

From the 1917 diary of Olga Romanov:

Mordvinov. Friday. **27 January**. To Znamenie and
we 2 to the infirmary. Bleshenkov had surgery.
Removed shrapnel and sutured the hips with wire.
Wrote quite a lot. Ritka too. Hauled breakfasts and
helped make the beds. Golitzyn came by. He is ill.
Mordvinov had breakfast and will have dinner. We 2
with Mama received three Americans, from the inactive
automobile-medical regiments. After that, she was
lying down on the balcony. We walked a little,
with Papa, and he went to work on the
tower. Wonderfully sunny, warm—virtually a spring
day. In the evening when it got dark, 1 [degree] of
frost. After tea, cinematograph. [We] teased
and tormented Mordvinov in the halls. Early to bed.

From the 1917 diary of Olga Romanov:

Count Zamoisky. Saturday. **28th January**. Directly to the infirmary, we 2. Wrote, made the beds and distributed medications, etc. Popov will be getting weight extensions. Unexpectedly, came over: Irakliy Vachnadze, Kiknadze, Kasyanov, Chernyatsov (from Evpatoria) and Adamka. As usual noisy, charming and cheerful. Bibi wrote with him to Mitya. Ate altogether. Walked with Papa, 2 [degrees] of frost. Later he dug at the tower, while we 4 came to the ruins [illegible] with skis and raced around the garden. Tumbled down constantly, of course. After tea at Al.[exei]'s, cinematograph, and after that with Papa to vsenoshnaya. Mama [came] later. Count Zamoisky had

dinner. After that, Shvybz and I rode in the sleigh [...].
Papa assembled a puzzle. After 11 o'clock to bed.
Yesterday before dinner we rode in the troika[46] with
Shura.

From the 1916 diary of Alexei Romanov:

29 January. Got up early. Studied and took a walk.
Had breakfast with Mama we 5. Walked during the
day and sledded. Papa sent a telegraph. [He] saw lots
of troops. At 5 o'cl. was at Mama's for tea. Had dinner
at 6 o'cl. Prepared homework. At 8 o'cl. was at
Mama's for dinner. Went to bed late. Nagorny's[47]
wallet was stolen with 90 rubles.

---

[46] Carriage drawn by three horses.
[47] Klementy Gregorievich Nagorny, Alexei's sailor nanny.

Letter from Anastasia to Nicholas II:

30 January, 1915. Tsarskoe Selo. My dear Papa Darling! I thank you very much for the kisses. I write to you so seldom, but [it is because I do not have] enough time. We just got back from riding. I taught Ortipo to "serve" and today to give paw, she does is so well, the darling. Now we will go to our infirmary. In the morning we went to Anya's. The nurses Olga and Tatiana went to Petrograd. Tatiana Andreyevna, the one with Aunt [Olga], she wrote to me that when you were at Aunt's you smoked a cigarette, she kept it and gave the ashes to the officers, and the ashtray was hers. Uncle Petya[48] had breakfast with us. I am happy that I will see you soon. I give you a very big kiss. Your loving daughter, 13-year-old Nastasia.

---

[48] Duke Peter Alexandrovich of Oldenburg, first husband of Grand Duchess Olga Alexandrovna.

Shvybzik. ANRIKZS. May God keep you. Sleep well.

From the 1917 diary of Michael Alexandrovich

31 January. Tuesday. Nadvornaya and departure to
Kamenetz-Podolsk. At 11 o'cl I made a farewell review
of the 1st brigade of the 9th Calvary division which
was lined up between Nadvornaya and Pnyuv. At
Nadvornaya on a wide street were lined up: my convoy
squadron, the 7th Samokratny company and all the
teams of our corps, and besides that all the staff
officers and officials—in the line-up there were 490
lower ranks, but only 42 of officers and officials. After
the farewell and awards of Georgievsky medals they all
marched ceremonially. To breakfast came: Nikitin (he

is now serving at headquarters of VII army), Semenov, Colonel Davydov and Ivanenko. At 3 o'cl I took photos with the entire staff, after which Vyazemsky and I took a walk towards Bystritza. Then I took photos with my convoy—also dropped by to see the chancery rooms, and dropped by to see Yuzefovich and Prince Begildeyev. At 4 3/4 had tea. At 8 o'cl I had dinner for the entire staff, besides officers there were officials too, altogether there were around 50 of us. Dinner took place in a former little restaurant along with a cinematograph, on the walls canvas and multicolored materials were stretched, everything was very nicely decorated. I sat between Yakov D and Prince Begildeyev. I had to give a farewell speech. Prince B, Yuzefovich and Angelov also spoke. Trumpeters of the Kazan regiment played. After dinner we went to the cinematograph. At 10 3/4 we drove off to the train station, everyone saw me off, along with convoy squadron with trumpeters—it was touching and sad. Going with me are: Yuzefovich, Vrangel, Vyazemsky and Colonel Daragan of the Bugsky regiment. The weather was sunny, [snow] melted, 2° of frost in the shade.

FEBRUARY

From the 1917 diary of Olga Romanov:

Count Zamoisky. Wednesday. **1st Feb.** In the
morning, we 2 to the infirmary. Pop[ov] had surgery of
the finger and clavicle. Strong pain, also Popov with
[illegible] and Poturev. [I] changed their ice,
distributed medicine, fixed the beds, set up Nikolaev,

etc., wrote. Dzhenkovich is fine, coughing. Koraikozov stopped by. Ate altogether. 2 [degrees] of frost. Alternately sunny with snow and storm. Went to the Grand Palace, after that to the ruins. In sleds and skis raced around across the garden. Met up with Papa and M. who were walking, and we switched with her. [I] walked with Papa, he was going to a reception, and the four of us walked on. After tea, cinematograph at Al.[exei]'s. At about 7 o'clock, rode with Papa to the vsenoshnaya. Mama later. AleksKonst[49] from the escort was there. In the evening, pasted in my album with M. Papa read Chekhov's "Tragic," "The Martyred Ones" and "The Eve Before Lent." At 11 o'clock to bed. Right now, it is 8 degrees of frost and a heavy snow storm.

---

[49] Alexander Konstantinovich Shvedov, an officer in the tsar's Escort Guard.

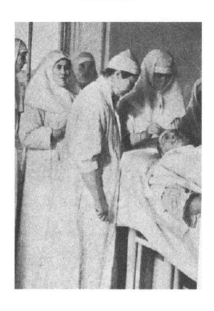

Mordvinov. Thursday. **2nd February**. All of us [went] with Papa to obednya. Mama [came] later. Dear Aleksei Konst.[antinovich]. Met up with [illegible] of the escort. Mordvinov had breakfast. After 'tomleniye' [did] the puzzle and the deputation of 1st Grebensky Kislyar. Papa's regiment. He was the hetman of Cherkessky, blue beshmet.[50] Sunny, 12 deg. frost. Walked on skis for about 2 ½ hrs, and around 4 o'clock went to Feodorovsky Sobor,[51] where 2 Sidorovsky Cossachkas [wives of Cossacks] arrived, Nina and Ludmila. And we came down with them sitting and standing [...] Lots of fun, returned by 5 o'clock. Al.[exei] is not [feeling] badly. In the evening

---

[50] Overcoat with no buttons.
[51] Feodorovsky Cathedral.

horsed around with Mordvinov in the halls. Early to bed. Mama went to Anya's infirmary at vsenoshnaya.

From the 1916 diary of Maria Romanov:

3 February. Had lessons in the morning. Breakfast 5 and Mama on the couch. Went to our infirmary with Anya. Rode with A. and Shura. Had tea with Mama and A. and Anya. Did homework. Had a French reading [lesson]. Had dinner 4 with Mama on the couch. Anya was here. Our [army] took [the town of] Yerzerum.

From the 1913 diary of Olga Romanov:

Monday. **4 February**. Had lessons. Had breakfast with Papa, Mama and Petrovsky. Mama sat at the table for the first time, went out on the balcony. In the afternoon [we] skied down the hill in the garden with Papa. The weather was wonderful—sunny and warm. Alexei also came [with us]. Had dinner with Papa and Mama and went to bed early.

From the 1916 diary of Maria Romanov:

5 February. Had lessons. Rode with Shura.
Breakfast 4 and Mama on the couch. Al. was in bed
all day. Went to a concert at our infirmary with
A.[nastasia]. Morfesi was there and also Sasha
Makarov and De Lazari played the guitar. One of them
played the accordion. In the afternoon had tea 4 with
Mama and Anya. Rode with O., T. and Shura. Had a
music [lesson]. Had dinner 4 with Mama in the
playroom. Anya was here.

From 1917 diary of Olga Romanov:

Count Kutaisov. Monday. **6th Feb.** We 2 to the infirmary. Everything is fine there. Wrote, distributed medicines, fed Pop[ov], etc. Kiknadze and B[illegible] came by. Biserov went to Odessa, while Cherepahov is planning [to go] to Chelyabinsk. Dzhurkovich is not bad. Kutaisov had breakfast. We 2 sat home with Al.[exei] in the playroom with Mama and Anya. [Illegible]. Uncle Mimi had tea. Very cold, bright and Papa [is] in a Plastun cherkesska.[52] Kutaisov had dinner and stayed rather long, putting together a puzzle. Papa read "Avgusteishiye Kadetsvo," "Pro-Dedushku." Very charming. At 11 o'clock to bed.

---

[52] Uniform of the infantry Cossacks.

From the 1917 diary of Nicholas II

7th February. Tuesday. Frosty day. From 10 ½ received: Gurko, Belyaev, the new Japanese—after that Ushid with the embassy and Pokrovsky. Svechin (dut.) had breakfast. Took a walk alone. At 6 o'cl. Uncle Pavel came over with the report. Read and wrote. Spent the evening all together.

From the 1913 diary of Tatiana Romanov:

8th February. Friday. Had lessons in the morning. Had breakfast four with Mama, Papa and U.[ncle] Georgi[53]. In the afternoon skied down the hill. Mama and Alexei were there too. Had tea with Trina. Had a French lesson, and then Papa, Olga and I went to the theater. The opera, Lohengrin. Wonderfully nice, and I liked it a lot. Golska sang. Returned at 12 ¾. Went to bed.

---

[53] Grand Duke Georgiy Mikhailovich, one of the imperial cousins.

From the 1916 diary of Maria Romanov:

9 February. Had lessons in the morning. Breakfast 4 with Papa, and Mama on the couch. Had a lesson in the afternoon. Went 4 to the Grand Palace. Rode in the troika 4 with Isa. Had tea 4 with Mama and Anya. Had a music [lesson]. Went to Zhylik's[54] concert at the gymnasium. Had dinner 4 with Papa, and Mama on the couch. Anya was here. Pasted in the album with Papa.

---

[54] Nickname of the imperial children's French tutor, Pierre Gilliard.

From the 1913 diary of Olga Romanov:

Sunday. **10 February**. Went to obednya at 10 ½.
After that [we] had a big breakfast. At 2 o'cl. 7 min. we
4 and Olga Yevgenievna Butsova went to Petersburg to
[see] Grandmama at Anichkov. After 3 o'cl. Aunt Olga
took us to her [house]. Shangin came over there too.
At about 3 ½ M.L. Tzigern-Shternberg and AKSHV
came over there too and then—Skvortsov, Irina, Zoya,
G. of Leichtenberg with Sasha and Nadya, N.N.
Rodionov, V.V. Khvoshinsky, S.S. Klyucharev and N.A.
Kulikovsky[55]. [We] had tea, and then played in the

---

[55] Nikolai Alexandrovich Kulikovsky, eventually the second husband of Grand
Duchess Olga Alexandrovna

large sitting room: cat and mouse, turkey, the ring, and also hide-and-seek downstairs in the dark. At dinner I sat with Tzigern-Sternberg and AKSHV. After that we went to the circus. Aunt Olga, K. Gagarin, Nadya, Klyucharev, Kulikovsky and 3 Cossacks. I sat with AKSHV[56] the whole time and fell deeply in love with him. May the Lord keep us. Saw him all day long—at obednya and at breakfast, also in the afternoon and the evening. It was so nice and fun. He is so sweet. Came home with Lili Obolenskaya after 12 o'cl. Mama had a headache in the morning, and her heart was No.1-1½ . Alexei's right arm hurts. Papa saw "Inspector General's Crooked Mirror" at the Chinese Theater. Thank you, God for this day.

---

[56] Alexander Konstantinovich Shvedov, an officer in the tsar's Escort Guard

From the 1917 diary of Olga Romanov:

Petrovsky. Saturday. **11ᵗʰ February**. Te° 37,2 – 37,6 – 38,0. – Until 12 o'clock [I was] lying down in daybed. Mama came by while Polyakov[57] was examining me. Until after dinner [was] lying down in the Red Room. During the day, Ritka[58] sat with me and had tea. Al. came in [his] bed for breakfast. Such a darling. [...] Ear hurts. Mama and Papa came by in the evening.

---

[57] One of the imperial physicians.
[58] Nickname for Margarita Sergeyevna Khitrovo.

Sunday. **12th February.** Until 12 o'clock in bed. Then Polyakov and to the Red Room. 37,5 – 37,7 – 37,7 – 37,6. Al., Lyolya and Zhenya had breakfast with me and were here during the day. [They were] cheerful. Mama sat for a long time and Anya. Papa stopped by. In the evening they came again before Gulesov. Nyuta[59] read to me.

---

[59] Anna Stepanovna Demidova, a maid in the service of the empress.

From the 1913 diary of Tatiana Romanov:

Tuesday. **12 February.** Had lessons in the morning.
Four had breakfast with Papa, Mama and U.[ncle]
Petya and A.[unt] Olga, and had tea with the same. In
the afternoon stayed here. Had a music lesson. Had
dinner with Papa, Mama and Uncle Petya. Later Papa
read to us. Went to bed at 10 o/cl.

From the 1913 diary of Olga Romanov:

Wednesday. **13 February**. Had lessons. Papa went to a reception in Petersburg. Mama does not feel well. Enlarged heart and tired. In the afternoon [we] skied down the hill with Nastasia. Papa returned at about 4 o'cl. and skied with us. Made us laugh. Had dinner with Papa and Mama. In the evening played kolorito[60] with Mama. Went to bed at 10 o'cl. 5 min. Bekker[61] came.

---

[60] A game
[61] Olga is referring to her menstrual period

From the 1917 diary of Olga Romanov:

Mordvinov. Tuesday. **14 Feb.** Slept well. Polyakov was here, and [made] a warm compress. [I] was lying down on the sofa all day. Mama sat during the day and Anya. Papa stopped by. After tea, Bibi sat with me, then N.P.—Nyuta read. T° – 37,1 – 37,2 ½ – 37,2 – 37,4 – In the evening Mama, Papa, N.P. and Mordvinov came by.

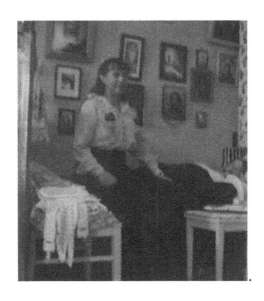

Letter from Anastasia to Nicholas II:

15 February, 1916. Tsarskoe Selo. My Precious Papa Darling. It is so pleasant that the sun came out today, it has not been out for a long time. Yesterday we three little ones, so to speak, went to Anya's infirmary where they had a concert. It was really nice. One little 10-year-old girl danced the Russian [dance] with an accordion, it was so sweet, and I felt sorry for her. Delaware and Yu. Morfesi, Sasha Makarov and your friend Larky were there as usual. He talked about an art lesson, it was so incredibly funny that the soldiers were crying from laughter. Then he talked about how you can hear the piano being played on three floors, also rather funny, and finally about the zoo, how they explain all the animals, etc. Nikolai Dmitrievich[62] was also there, and Irina Tolstaya. While Olga and Tatiana were at their infirmary at this time, and they also had a concert. Fersen Bezobrazov and various young ladies played the balalaikas there, and many others. So, you think we are not going to [another] concert, right? You are mistaken, we are going to the Grand Palace, where they will have something like a comedy of the crooked mirror, so we are going there as they begged us desperately. "Sleep the achievement of pride, everyone sleep." Now I will have the arithmetic lesson. Maria and Alexei have colds and they don't go out except to the infirmaries. Well I will end. I send you an awfully big kiss. Regards to yours. Your loving loyal and faithful Kaspiyitz.[63]

---

[62] Nikolai Dmitrievich Demenkov, Grand Duchess Maria's romantic crush.
[63] Refers to the 148th Kaspiyitzky Infantry *Regiment, of which Anastasia was honorary colonel.*

From the 1917 diary of Nicholas II

16th February. Thursday. From 10 o'cl. received: Ilyin, Kochubei and Mosolov. At 11 ½ went to the clock [?]. N.P. had breakfast and dinner. Sat at Olga's, Maria's and Alexei's. Took a walk with Tatiana and Anastasia. It was 5° of frost and quiet. At 9 ½ received Protopopov.

From the 1917 diary of Michael Alexandrovich

17 February. Friday. Gatchina[64]. Got up like all the other days, late and at 11 o'cl went to church. Before breakfast Natasha[65] and I took a walk around the garden. At 2 1/2 I took a ride astride Vityaz, rode around Priorat, and at 3 3/4 Natasha and I took a sleigh ride across Priorat to the Black Gate, and then to Kurakinsky and home. At 5 o'cl Prince Kantakuzin, Commander of the equestrian artillery of the 9th cavalry division, arrived. Around 5 1/2 Alyosha arrived, and at 6 o'cl we went to the palace for a service, after which we confessed to Father Strakhov. After dinner Alyosha studied for a bit. The weather

---

[64] The Gatchina Palace.
[65] Countess Natalia Brasova, Grand Duke Michael's wife.

was sunny, wonderful lighting, in the afternoon 11°, and in the evening 17°.

Postcard from Olga to V.I. Chebotareva:

18-II [February] 1917. Dear Valentina Ivanovna![66] I am thinking of You today and kiss [you] very affectionately. May the Lord keep Your Grisha.[67] Sister O. Romanova

---

[66] Valentina Ivanovna Chebotareva, a fellow nurse and friend to the grand duchesses
[67] V.I. Chebotareva's son, Grigori

From the 1916 diary of Maria Romanov:

20 February. Rode with A. and Shura. Walked-skipped with A. Breakfast 5 with Papa and Mama and 2 Englishmen. In the afternoon built the tower 4 with Papa and the sailors. Went to our infirmary with A. Sat with Sh.[akh]-N.[Nazarov]. Had tea with Papa, Mama and Uncle Pavel. Went to Vsenoshnaya 4 with Papa. Had dinner with the same with Mama on the couch. Papa read, Anya was here.

From the 1917 diary of Nicholas II:

19th February. Sunday. At 10 ½ went to obednya with Tatiana, Anastasia also has a cold. Vilkitsky had breakfast and dinner. Took a walk alone. Recevied Balashov- member of the Duma, before tea. There was a cinematograph at 6 o'cl – saw the end of the "Mysterious hand". In the evening [the following] gathered at Alix's: Llili Dehn, N.P., Myasoyedov-Ivanov, Rodionov and Kublitsky.

From the 1917 diary of Olga Romanov:

Petrovsky. Tuesday. **21st February**. Was lying down until after 12 o'clock, had breakfast in bed; until after dinner in the Red Room, around 2 o'clock Elena came over and sat for a bit. She was in Elizavetgrad, Voznesensk and Odessa. Saw the Serbian refugees and the division. After that, Polyakov. Papa stopped by before his walk. Mama sat until 4 o'clock when AlekKonst. and Viktor came. We sat together until 5 ½ o'clock, so nice and cozy. Talked a lot. Shurik[68] is going to Mogilev with Papa tomorrow. T° 36,3- 37,1 –

---

[68] Most likely Alexander Kostantinovich Shvedov.

36,9 ¾ – Bibi received a lovely, nice letter from Mitya.[69] [illegible] Tat.[iana] does not go to the infirmary, we are quarantined this week due to the measles, which Lyolya Makarov was ill with. In the evening Mama and Papa came by. Anya too.

From the 1916 diary of Maria Romanov:

22 February. Had lessons. Then went to church 5 with Papa. Breakfast with same, with Vikitsky and Mama on the couch. In the afternoon went to our infirmary with A. Sat with Sh.N. Walked 5 with Papa, built and jumped off the tower[70]. Had tea in the

---

[69] Dmitri Shakh-Bagov, a wounded soldier and Olga's love interest during the war years.
[70] Snow fort they built in Alexander Park

playroom. Had an English lesson. Went to church 5 with Papa and Mama. Had dinner with same except Al. Papa read, Anya was here.

23 February. Had lessons. Went to church 5 with Papa. Breakfast with same, with Count Sheremetiev and Mama on the couch. Built the tower, and jumped from it. Had tea in the playroom. Had music. Went to church 5 with Papa and Mama. Had dinner 4 with Papa, Count Sheremetiev and Mama on the couch. Papa read, Anya was here.

From the 1913 diary of Maria Romanov:

24 February. Monday. In the morning I stayed in bed. Had breakfast four with Papa, Sergei and Mama on the sofa. In the afternoon I stayed home and Trina read. Had a music lesson. Had tea with Papa and Mama. Did homework. Had dinner with Anastasia.

From the 1916 diary of Maria Romanov:

25 February. Lessons as usual. Went to church 5 with Papa. Breakfast with same and Mama on the sofa. Built the tower. Went to our infirmary with A., sat with Sh.N. Had tea with Papa, Mama and O. and A. Went to church 5 with Papa and Mama. Had dinner with same except Al. Papa read. Anya was here.

From the 1917 diary of Nicholas II

26th February. Sunday. At 10 o'cl. went to obednya. Report ended in time. Lots of people had breakfast and all the foreigners. Wrote to Alix and drove on the Bobruisky highway to the chapel, where took a walk. The weather was clear and frosty. After tea, read and received sen.[ator] Tregobov before dinner. In the evening played some dominoes.

27th February. Monday. Riots began in Petrograd a few days ago; unfortunately, the military started to take part in them. What an awful feeling to be so far away and receive only snippets of bad news! Stayed for the report for a while. During the day took a walk on the highway to Orsha. The weather was sunny. After dinner decided to leave for T.[sarskoe] S.[elo] as soon as possible and moved into the train at one in the morning.

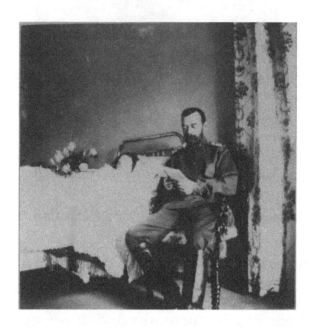

From the 1913 diary of Nicholas II

27 February. Wednesday. Tatiana's illness[71] is coming along normally. From 10 o'cl. until 11 1/4 received Maklakov. Went to a pre-sanctified obednya.[72] Zhitkevich (on duty) had breakfast—he is now the commander of the 70th Ryazhsky regiment.

---

[71] Tatiana contracted typhoid in early 1913.
[72] Pre-sanctified obednya refers to a liturgy service that happens regularly during Great Lent. Communicants receive Communion of the Gifts which were sanctified the previous Sunday.

From 2 o'clock until 4 1/2 o'cl. had a nice workout with the daughters at the ice rink—we started building the big tower. After tea, read. Same in the evening.

From the 1905 diary of Nicholas II

28 February. Monday. Started to prepare for Communion at the camp church. Ernie and his wife went to the city. Uncle Aleksei[73] had breakfast. Then I had military deliberations on the question of Kuropatkin. Involved were: U.[ncle] Aleksei, Nikolasha,[74] Dragomirov, count Vorontzov,

---

[73] Grand Duke Aleksei Alexandrovich.
[74] Grand Duke Nikolai Nikolaevich "the Younger."

Fredericks,[75] Gesse, Sukhomlinov, Roop and Komarov. Took a walk, [snow was] melting.

From the 1916 diary of Maria Romanov:

29 February. Had lessons. Breakfast 5 with Papa, Uncle Georgiy[76] and Ioann. In the afternoon went to our infirmary with A. Sat with M.Z. Baron, Ton, and A.V. Walked and built the tower. Had tea with A. and T. in the playroom. Had English and music lessons. Did homework. Dinner 3 with Papa, Ioann and Dmitri.[77] Papa read, Anya was here. Mama has neuralgia, and she stayed in bed almost the entire day.

---

[75] Count Vladimir Borisovich Fredericks, the imperial household minister.
[76] Grand Duke Georgiy Mikhailovich.
[77] Grand Duke Dmitri Pavlovich, first cousin of the tsar.

MARCH

From the 1915 diary of Nicholas II:

1 March. Sunday. Not far from Baranovichi caught up with two trains with the troops, which I reviewed. At 12 ½ arrived at Stavka.[78] Before breakfast received

---

[78] Military headquarters in Mogilev.

Nikolasha.[79] After the meal, there was a short report. Went outside and took a really nice walk through the woods and fields. The weather remained spring-like and the sun warmed one pleasantly. After tea received Georgiy for a long report about the Caucasus. Read the entire evening; had tea with everyone.

From the 1913 diary of Nicholas II:

2nd March. Saturday. Today we had the chance to receive Holy Communion. By the end of obednya Kedrinsky walked up to Tatiana's [room] and also gave her communion! She was not feeling too badly and slept for two hours during the day. Took a walk until

---

[79] Grand Duke Nicholas Nikolaevich.

12 o'cl; it rained all day. Received Count Fredericks with a report. He had breakfast with us. Olga arrived; worked at the tower and took a walk. At 6 ½ went to the dear regiment church. After dinner studied and read.

1916 letter from Maria to Nicholas II:

3 March. My sweet and dear Papa! Yesterday after we saw you off, Tatiana, Anastasia and I went to the cemetery in a motor. We drove there for an unusually long time because the roads are so bad. We arrived there and went to the officers' graves, there was nothing there yet, and too much snow, then I wanted to visit the graves of our patients from the lower ranks. There was a big pile of snow on the side of the road, so

I was able to climb up with great difficulty on my knees and jump down from it. Down there the snow turned out to be above the knees, and although I was wearing long boots, I was already wet so I decided to continue ahead. Nearby I found one grave with the surname Mishenko, this was the name of our patient; I laid down some flowers there and walked ahead, and suddenly I saw the same surname again, I looked up at the board, [to see] which regiment he was from, and it turned out that he was one of our patients [too], but not the same one. So I laid down the flowers for him and was just starting to walk away when I fell on my back, and was lying there for almost a minute not knowing how to get up, there was so much snow that I could not reach the ground with my hand for leverage. I finally got up and walked ahead. Earlier Tatiana and Anastasia said that they were going to go to another cemetery, to Sonia Orbeliani[80] [grave] and that they will return for me. But instead they sent the man in charge of the graveyard to help me. He crawled over to me with great difficulty and we went to look for another grave together. We searched and searched and could not understand at all what happened to it. It turned out that it was closer to the fence and that

---

[80] Sonia Orbeliani was a Georgian princess and friend of the imperial family.

we should have climbed over a ditch. He stood in the ditch and said to me "I will carry you over", I said "no", he said "let's try." Of course, he put me down not on the other side but right in the middle of the ditch. And so, we are both standing in the ditch, up to our bellies in snow, and dying from laughter. It was hard for him to climb out, as the ditch was deep, and for me too. So, he climbed out somehow and stretched his hands out to me. Of course, I slid back down into the ditch on my stomach about three times, but finally climbed out. And we performed all this with flowers in our hands. Then we couldn't fit through between the crosses for a while, as we were both wearing our coats. But in the end, I did find the grave. Finally, we were able to leave the cemetery. Tatiana and Anastasia were already waiting for me on the road. I felt half-dead from heat and dampness. We climbed into the motors and drove away. I took off one boot to shake out the snow. At this same time, we ran into a wagon. We were driving rather fast. We just swerved to the side a little, when Lapin's steering wheel spun [out of control] and our front tires slid into a snow bank, and scarily [we] turned to our side, I jumped out wearing one boot and put the other one back on out on the road. What could we do, no one was there anymore and it was already 1 o'clock 10 minutes. Then we 3 decided to walk home on foot, but luckily at this moment some squadron was walking back from shooting practice and they dug out the motor, while we walked almost all the way to the shooting gallery. The motor caught up to us and we got home safely. But the road was so bad the entire time that we were certain that the motor would break. Across from the Cuirassier Cathedral. And we were tossed up so high that Tatiana almost hit her head on the roof. In the afternoon during our troika ride we almost ran over another sleigh. So, after all this, we went to our infirmary, and we were certain that we will fall into a ditch or something else will happen to us again. [We] went to the tower yesterday. The sailors were all very sweet and worked hard. You were very much missed there. [...] In the evening Anya finished reading "Our People Abroad" to us. Olga went to bed early of course. And you are probably enjoying the English book. Grandmama sent the book "Olive," and Mama sent her another one. Well, farewell my darling. May Christ be with you. +   Your Kazanetz[81]. I kiss you affectionately and squeeze you a lot and for a long

---

[81] Refers to the 5th Kazansky Dragoons regiment, of which Maria was honorary captain.

time. Titanis, titanis. Dukchik Dukchik.

From the 1913 diary of Nicholas II:

4th March. Monday. The day remained warm, snowing occasionally. [I] was busy from 10 o'cl. until one. After breakfast at 2 1/2 went to the palace grounds with the children. Reviewed the young sailors of the 1st and 2nd mine divisions and underwater regiment. Fabritzky[82] is their commander. Was satisfied with all. Returned home at 3 1/2 and went to take a walk. Sat with Tatiana until tea. At 6 o'cl. received Scheglovitov. After dinner studied for a long time.

---

[82] Rear-admiral Semyon Semyonovich Fabritzky.

From 1916 diary of Alexei Romanov:

5 March. Got up early. Studied and took a walk. Had breakfast we 5 with Mama. In the afternoon took a walk with Kolya. Had tea and dinner at Mama's. Had dinner at 6 o'cl. Went to bed early.

6 March. Got up early. Took a walk. Had breakfast with Mama, O., T., M. and A. Took a walk in the afternoon. Went to obednya. Had dinner at Mama's. Went to Anya's infirmary, a magician was there. Had dinner at 6 o'cl. Went to bed early.

From the 1916 diary of Maria Romanov:

7 March. Had lessons. Rode with Shura, breakfast 5 with Mama on the sofa. Went to our infirmary with A. Ivan bid farewell to us as he is leaving from the Svodny regiment and returning to the Black Sea. Went to Vitebsk community infirmary with Isa, in the barracks of the 3rd St. Regiment. Had tea 4 with Mama and Anya. Had English and music lessons. Rode in a troika with O., A. and Shura. Had dinner 4 and Mama on the sofa. Lili Dehn[83] with [her] husband, Anya and Baron Taube were here. Sat and looked at a [photo] album, then went to tea. It was very cozy.

---

[83] Lady-in-waiting Yulia Alexandrovna Dehn.

From the 1913 diary of Nicholas II:

8th March. Friday. The morning was busy.
Between reports 30 bankers from Petersburg and
Moscow presented themselves to me and Alix,
[they] brought us a million rubles to commemorate the
300th anniversary [of Romanov Dynasty]—for charity.
After breakfast, took a walk with three daughters;
there was slush from [both] the top and the bottom.
Before tea received Gen.[eral] Adj[utant] Ivanov, after
tea Langov. Managed to finish the paperwork before 7
1/2. Went to Mama's and had dinner with her. At 10
1/2 returned to T.S.

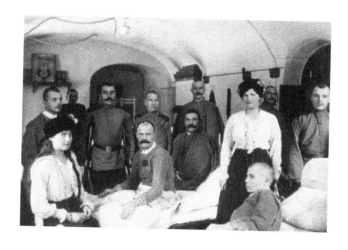

1916 letter from Maria to Nicholas II:

9 March. My dear darling Papa! Today is Spring already, but it's 7 [degrees below] here and snowing with wind. Completely unacceptable. [I] just finished breakfast. Olga and Tatiana are going to Petrograd for charities and committee, and will have tea at Grandmama's, and will also stop by Aunt Ksenia's who feels terrible and does not leave the house. I will now go to our infirmary with A. Nikolai Dmitrievich[84] bade farewell to Mama. Before that, the regiment had a goodbye party for him in the evening at 7 o'clock, which only ended at 5 in the morning, so Resin looked rather sad, and when he was leaving the room [he] almost knocked over a vase with flowers, and his voice was not very nice either. But N.D. himself was very

---

[84] Demenkov, Maria's favourite officer

charming. I have not seen him since then, and don't even expect to anymore. Right now, Anastasia is sitting here and playing the balalaika. Well so long, my dear. I kiss you affectionately and apologize for a boring letter. Your Kazanetz. May Christ be with you.

+

From 1916 diary of Alexei Romanov:

10 March. Got up at 8 ½ studied and took a walk. Had breakfast with Mama and the sisters. In the afternoon took a walk and worked. Did homework. Had dinner at 6 o'cl. Went to Mama's for dinner. Went to bed as usual.

From the 1913 diary of Nicholas II:

11th March. Monday. The entire day was quiet and foggy. Between reports received Delkasse, [who was] appointed here as an ambassador. At 2 1/2 the second naval recruits review took place on the Palace Square. They came from Revel and Sveaborg—from a brigade of cruisers and the Battleship Brigade. They presented as fine lads. Walked for a bit. At 4 1/2 Georgiy arrived; had tea with him. Read a lot. In the evening, out loud.

From 1916 diary of Alexei Romanov:

12 March. Got up early. Studied and took a walk. Had breakfast with Mama, O., T., M. and A. Took a walk in the afternoon. Titi[85] was here. Went to tea at Mama's and dinner. Had dinner at 6 o'cl. Went to bed early. ~~Yesterday it was~~ It was raining.

---

[85] Lili Dehn's son.

From the 1913 diary of Nicholas II:

13th March. Wednesday. Excellent sunny day. At 10 1/2 went to the city to the reception at the Winter Palace. Had breakfast at Mama's. Returned at 3 1/4 and from the station walked directly to work on [breaking] ice. Marie helped me. Before tea sat with Tatiana as usual. At 6 o'cl. received Maklakov. Finished paperwork before 8 o'cl. After dinner went to the other side [of the palace] and looked at porcelain.

From the 1914 diary of Nicholas II:

14 March. Friday. In the morning read quietly and took a little walk. All was melting, but at times it was snowing. After Bark's report, received 10 governors and leaders of the nobility. At 2 1/2 bid farewell in front of the Alexander Palace 365 [troops] leaving for the reserves and reviewed 431 newly arrived ranks. of the Svodny Regiment. Broke the ice on the rink around our tower. At 6 o'cl. received Scherbatov. Bathed with Alexei in my bath. In the evening we sat with Grigori.

From the 1918 diary of Nicholas II

2/15 March[86]**.** Friday. Remembering these days last year in Pskov and in the train! How much longer will our poor motherland be tormented and pulled apart by the external and internal enemies? Sometimes it seems that there is no more strength to take this, I don't even know what to hope or wish for? Nevertheless, there is no one like God! May His holy will be served!

---

[86] Old/new style dates. In 1918 the new government implemented the new style dates in Russia to match the rest of Europe.

From the 1913 diary Nicholas II:

16th March. Saturday. Was busy from 10 o'cl. until one. Did not take a walk. At breakfast were: Olga, Gavriil (on duty) and Fredericks. Both received Prince Golitzyn, Ditz and a deputation of huntsmen with congratulation for the 300th anniversary [of Romanov Dynasty]. Worked on ice with Marie. Towards the end Alexei came with V.N. Derevenko, like yesterday. After tea, read for a bit and at 6 1/2 went to vsenoshnaya with the removal of the Holy Cross. Archmandrite Shavelsky performed the service. In the evening studied for a long time.

From the 1916 diary of Alexei Romanov:

17 March. Got up early. Studied and took a walk. Had breakfast with Mama, O., T., M. and A. Took a walk in the afternoon. Went to Mama's for tea and dinner. Had dinner at 6 o'cl. Anya was at dinner

From the 1913 diary of Olga Romanov:

Monday. **18 March.** Had lessons. Had breakfast and dinner with Papa, Mama and Kostya. In the afternoon went to review the 1st Baltic Navy Crew. It was very nice. 18 degrees in the sun, so warm. N.P. and a few other officers from the yacht were there. T. is fine. Now Trina is sick. Alexei stayed in bed. In the evening Papa read reports by K. Ad. Petrov from Sevastopol and by K. Gr. Vorozheikin from "The Russia" [...]. Mama and I worked.

From the 1915 diary of Tatiana Romanov:

Thursday, **19 March.** At 9 o'clock went to church for communion. Alexei was in bed, had communion at home. Then all had tea upstairs. Breakfast, tea, and lunch with Papa and Mama. In the afternoon skated 4 with Isa. Then went to the Grand Palace. Went to church to twelve gospels. Mama was tired. Alexei's neck also hurts.

Dmitri Pavlovich to Nicholas II:

Palermo, **1914. 19th March.** My dear uncle, it's amazing isn't it that suddenly I decided to write to you—as you know all my love of this sort of sports. But living so terribly far away from friends and loved ones, sometimes one wants to talk and share one's thoughts. As it is now a complete impossibility for me to come to you on the 7.20 train for dinner at Tsarskoe, I decided to write to you, my dear, and write not just some silly "cartolina postale", but a real letter. Of course, my decision makes it worse for you, as a card can be read in one minute, while a letter, and one written by me at that—requires a lot more work and a good eye. But nevertheless. Take this message with you when you are shitting. The time will be more leisurely, and at the very least you can always wipe yourself with it (combine the pleasant with the practical). I stopped at Palermo, although the doctor said that I should live in Tower-Mine, but there, according to Papa, to live for a long period is unimaginable. No walks, the garden too small. And since the most important thing for my health—was the warmth and the sun, I headed to Sicily, where I am thinking to stay for another two or three weeks. From Petersburg I ended up in Paris, where I stayed for five days. I felt so weak that couldn't even think about evenings and holidays. I found Papa and the countess in good health; both are very busy with the move to Tsarskoe, which in their projection is supposed to happen at the end of April our style. From Paris I passed by Palermo, where I stopped at a good hotel, outside of the city, away from the city dust and noise. It was right on the beach, the terraces lead into the cliffs, and walking one can hear the soft caressing sounds of the waves. On the day of my arrival the weather was really bad, it was raining and phenomenally windy. Then the weather became wonderful, the wind continued for another three-four days, but now it is delightful. I am positively coming alive each day, got a tan, and cough is almost gone. The air is so amazing. In order to demonstrate graphically what life-giving air is here, it is enough to say that a month ago an Englishwoman arrived here. She was completely ill with nerves and so weak that could hardly stand on her legs. Now she is playing tennis, dancing and walking as much as she wants.

I was so insanely bored the first week. Although my most dear general Layming is with me, who takes care of me touchingly. About four days ago "count" and "countess" Kokovtzev arrived here. Such is my fate—I must always meet with the Kokovtzevs. We took a lot of interesting walks with them, and saw a lot of interesting things. Today we had a big outing in an automobile. Went to see the ruins of the old Greek cathedral and V century theater on the P.X. II. Well, walking around suddenly I remembered so terribly clearly our walks with you, and felt sorry that you do not know any of these views, and I wanted to speak and have a talk with you; but unfortunately, the only way to do it is—to write. Really forgive me.

Well, my health now is better thank God! The most pleasant thing—is that not only the physical health is improving but also emotional. During my stay in Petersburg this same emotional health plunged terribly. I became irritable and stupid. Lost command of myself—this is very unpleasant. Now je me retrouve. It must be so boring for you to read all this—I understand this, but I also understand that you are not completely indifferent to this.

I want to speak with you, and now, without thinking of what I was going to write, it is as if I am speaking with you, seeing you in front of me in your study at Tsarskoe, under the hanging lamp. I repeat, it is so pleasant for me to write to you, my dear, because I know and feel that you understand me. I am sending de temps en temps to Bologne, a dry health report and basta... ?!

A rather shiny Kokovtzev has a very energetic appearance, and as I already mentioned, he sees a lot.

The public here is very boring. One snout is worse than the next. Devil only knows what this is. And among all this rubbish lives a pair of professional dancers who hold séances every day during tea, and a French coquette who probably is looking for a patron. But when bird-less even an ass is a nightingale—as they say. There is a big very nice theater here—opera. They sing wonderfully well. About two-three days ago I went to a play and liked it a lot. And how are things by you? How was the meeting of the Romanian prince and Missy? How is her majesty's health? Tell her that I think of her often, drowning in helpless and unnecessary tears of passion, embrace my pillow thinking of her. John is a boy and a puppy compared to me. How is Alexei and the children? Hug Olga and the daughters for me please. Well, it is now time to end this short letter. Forgive me mine own, if you are sick of me. I embrace you tightly. Your sincere and deeply faithful

Dmitri

Maria[87] is now in Athens. I haven't had news from her since the day she left Petersburg.

---

[87] Grand Duke Dmitri's elder sister, Grand Duchess Maria Pavlovna "the Younger"

From the 1916 diary of Maria Romanov:

20 March. Went to church with Papa and Mama. Had breakfast 5, Papa and Mama on the sofa. 4 went to the Gr.[and] Pal.[ace]. Walked with Papa and Mama [rode] in a carriage. Broke ice 4 with Papa. Had tea in the playroom. 5 went to Anya's concert at the infirmary, "Ivanov Pavel" and the magicians. Went to our infirmaries with A., 17 soldiers arrived from the train. Rode with A. and Shura. Had dinner 5 with Papa, Mama, Silaev and Anya. Papa read.

From the 1913 diary of Maria Romanov:

21 March. Thursday. In the morning sledded with Madame Conrad.[88] Had lessons. Had breakfast with Papa and Mama on the sofa. In the afternoon broke ice with Papa. Had tea alone. Had a music [lesson]. Went to the lower regiment church.[89] Had dinner with Papa and Mama on the sofa.

---

[88] Wife of the music teacher of the imperial children.
[89] The imperial family's private chapel located in the cellar of the Feodorovsky Cathedral.

From the 1913 diary of Nicholas II:

21st March. Thursday. The same wonderful weather continues, but I was very busy from 10 o'cl. in the morning until half past one and did not go out in the garden. Tatiana came downstairs to Alix's for the first time and sat there until 6 o'cl. Worked on ice nicely with the rest of the daughters. Studied until 8 o'cl. In the evening [read] aloud.

From the 1913 diary of Olga Romanov:

Friday. **22 March**. At 9 o'cl. 45 min. we 3 went to
Petersburg with Papa to the Second All-Russian Craft
Exhibition. Stayed there for 2 hours, walked around,
looked at everything. Everything was interesting. Had
breakfast at Grandmama's with Uncle Petya, Aunt
Olga and Irina, who also went to the exhibition. After
we returned, broke ice with Papa in the garden. 8
degrees in the shade. It was foggy in the morning. Had
dinner with Papa, Mama and Dmitri. In the evening
played kolorito with Mama. She is not feeling well.
[Our] brother, T., Mikhail, Pavel had tea with them. T.
came downstairs and had dinner. Went to bed at 10
o'cl.

From the 1915 diary of Tatiana Romanov:

Monday, **23 March**. In the morning went to obednya. Then there was a procession of the cross around the church. Breakfast 5 with Papa, Mama and Uncle Pavel.[90] At 2 o'clock went to the Grand Palace for Easter greetings of the suite and soldiers. Mama took turns with Olga giving out eggs, and I helped. Dmitri was there. Then went downstairs to the infirmary, where Mama gave eggs to the officers. Nikolai Pavlovich was upstairs. Had tea with Papa and Mama.

---

[90] Grand Duke Pavel Alexandrovich, Grand Duke Dmitri's father.

Then Olga and I drove to [see] Tatiana[91] in Pavlovsk. The Yerevantzy Teriev with his wife and Snarsky were there, but they soon left. Then [I] sat with Tatiana, Olga played with Teymuraz[92]. Then went down for a moment to [see] Aunt and Uncle. Dinner with Mama and Papa at Grandmama's. Spoke on the telephone with Karangozov and Shalva Vachnadze. Saw a wounded volunteer at the Grand Palace, Archil Djordjadze, Tina-Tina's brother.

From the 1913 diary of Olga Romanov:

---

[91] Princess Tatiana Konstantinovna, eldest daughter of Grand Duke Konstantin Konstantinovich.
[92] Prince Teymuraz Bagration-Mukhransky, Princess Tatiana Konstantinovna's son.

Sunday. **24 March**. Went to obednya. Ioann R.'s choir sang. In the evening the entire imperial court went to vsenoshnaya. There was a big breakfast. Dear AKSHV was there, and also at the church. In the afternoon we broke the ice with Papa and Irina. 5 degrees. Had tea with Irina, Papa and Mama. T was also there. Had dinner with Papa, Mama and Prince Bagration. In the evening N.P. and Anya came over. Papa read in his [room]. Mama is not feeling well. It was cozy.

From 1916 diary of Alexei Romanov:

25 March. Got up early. Took a walk. Went to obednya. Had breakfast with Papa, Mama, O., T., M. and A. Took a walk in the afternoon. Dmitri had breakfast. Papa and Mama went to the city. Saw Papa off. Had dinner at 6 o'cl. Went to bed early. Was at Mama's for dinner.

From the 1916 diary of Maria Romanov:

26 March. Walked with Trina, had lessons, rode with Shura. Had breakfast 5 with Papa and Mama, Count Fredericks, and Count Kutaisov. Broke ice with Papa and the sailors. Mama was there. Papa departed, [we] saw him and Dmitri off. Had tea 4 and Mama. Went to vsenoshnaya 5 with Mama. Had dinner 4 and Mama on the sofa. Anya was here.

27 March. Sunday. Went to Church 5 with Mama, breakfast with same and Isa. Went to our infirmary with A. Rode 4 with Mama and Anya. Went to a concert at Anya's infirmary 5 with Mama. Rode 2 with Shura. Had dinner 4 and Mama on the sofa. Anya was here.

From the 1913 diary of Nicholas II:

28th March. Thursday. It snowed overnight. At 11 o'cl. went to the manege[93] with Olga A and the children for the church parade of the Svodny regiment. It was a brilliant and smart presentation. Breakfast with the ladies in our Circular Hall. Received several people. Took a walk and worked. At 6 o'cl. Sabler

---

[93] An arena or enclosed area where horses and riders are trained. In this case, an indoor riding arena at Tsarskoe Selo.

came over to [see] me, before tea Shirinsky-Sh[ikhmatov]. At 8 o'cl. went to dinner at the officer meeting of the Svodny Regiment. Played the pyramids with Poretsky. Then Plevitskaya sang, taking turns with Lersky and Paul Robert. They really made us laugh. Spent the time very nicely.

From the 1918 diary of Nicholas II:

29 March. Thursday. During the morning walk saw the "special commissar" Demianov, who with his assistant Degtyarev, escorted by the commandant and marksmen, made rounds of the guard house and the garden. Because of him, i.e. this Demianov, and the marksmen's unwillingness to miss him, was why the all the fuss started three days ago.

From the 1914 diary of Nicholas II:

30th March. Palm Sunday. Woke up to a happy sunny morning. At 10 o'cl. obednya started, then review of the command and early breakfast. At 12 1/2, [we] exited Sevastopol with a salute from the squadron and the fortress. "Almaz," "Kagul" escorted by four large destroyers. Across from Balaklav, the destroyer "Bespokoiny" caught up and passed us, with Grigorovich on the way to Yalta; ran into it again near Simeyiz, moving on average at 28 knot speed. Approached the mall at 4 o'cl. There awaiting us, among many others, were—Kostya, Mavra and Mitya—wonderful guard of honor—from my company of the Kabardinsky Regiment. Around 5 o'cl. [we]

disembarked from the yacht and headed to Livadia.[94] Here the sea was colder than in Sevastopol, despite the sun. All the fruit trees are blooming and many others are green. At the palace, the guard of honor—from my company of the Emperor Alexander III 16th sharpshooter regiment. Went to church for molebna. Had tea. Reviewed things burned and ruined by the fire in the freight train on the way here. Took a short walk around here, in Oreanda.[95] Unpacked my things and straightened up the rooms. Had dinner with O. and T. Such a blessing to be back in Crimea.

Letter from Anastasia to Nicholas II:

---

[94] Livadia Palace, located in the Crimea, was the summer retreat of the last tsar and his family.

[95] The Palace of Oreanda was built for Empress Alexandra Feodorovna, wife of Tsar Nicholas I. In 1860, ownership of the palace passed to Grand Duke Konstantin Nikolaevich, who lived there until the palace was destroyed by fire in 1882. The grand duke had no money to restore it, so the ruins were carefully maintained as a picturesque "Greek Ruin" amidst the elaborate gardens and were a beautiful spot to walk and rest.

31 March, 1916. T[sarskoe].S.[elo]. My precious Papa Darling. I am hurrying to write to you as we must go to the infirmary. Maria and I and Alexei had breakfast upstairs as Mama and the sisters are in Petrograd. We go outside and break ice. Yesterday Fedotov was not there. Krylov is terribly weak and showed up. Maria and I are now playing, she on the piano, and I on the balalaika, and it's turning out rather well, but it's even better with Olga. I am imagining how the 1st Hundred was happy to see you there in particular and I was a little envious of you. We will go break ice again today, and to two infirmaries, to ours and to the Grand Palace. I give you a terribly big kiss and squeeze you. Your loving loyal and faithful Kaspiyitz. +

APRIL

From the 1905 diary of Nicholas II:

1st April. Friday. In the morning received 20 wounded officers. Dabich (on duty) had breakfast with us. Took a walk with Irene, Maria and Dmitri. Then worked with him. The day was warm, but grey. Had tea at Mama's. In the evening received Bulygin.

Христосъ Воскресе!
Золотой мой, безцѣнный
Папа. Пошли Тебѣ
Господь тихо и ра-
достно встрѣтить
Свѣтлый праздникъ.
Крѣпко, ужасно
крѣпко Тебя, Папа
мой родной цѣлую.
Твой вѣрный
Пластунъ.
2. Апр. 1917. +

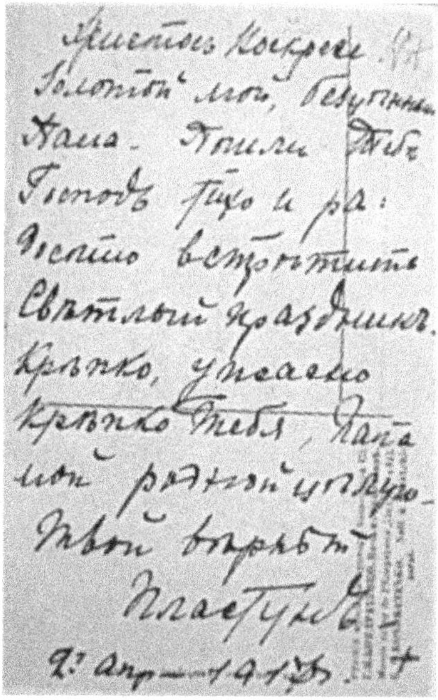

Easter card from Olga to Nicholas II:

Christ has risen! My Golden priceless Papa. May the Lord let You peacefully and happily greet this holy day. I send you an enormously affectionate kiss, my very own dear Papa. Your loyal Plastun. **2nd April, 1917**.

+

Letter from Alexei Romanov:

To Kolya (Tobolsk, **3 April, 1918**). Dear Niki, I am very grateful for the cannon. I hope that we will see each other soon. Regards to Mother, Grandmother and Fefer. My handwriting is bad because I am lying in bed. My leg hurts, but I think it will soon be better. Yours, Ieskela[96]

[On the reverse side, on top of the page Alexei wrote]: "I am sending you a prosfora.[97]"

---

[96] Alexei's name sounded out backwards.
[97] The host offered during Holy Liturgy.

From the 1913 diary of Olga Romanov:

Thursday. **4 April**. Had lessons. Had breakfast with Papa, Mama, Aunt Olga and G. In the afternoon Papa went to Petersburg. We walked with Aunt Olga and watched the Infantry regiment practice. Tatiana rode in a real carriage for the first time. It was over 10 degrees in the shade, very warm, feels like summer. Mama sat on the balcony. Aunt Olga and Papa had tea with her. Papa went to Grandmama's for dinner. Aunt Olga stayed until 9 and played kolorito with Mama.

From the 1915 diary of Nicholas II:

5th April. Sunday. At 9 ¼ arrived at Stavka. After a talk with Nikolasha [I] went to [hear] a report. At 10 ½ went to obednya. During the day took a walk around Baranovichi and saw the training of artillery leib-Cossacks team. Read, wrote and rested before dinner. In the evening played some dominos. The weather was cold, sunny, and it even snowed a bit.

From the 1913 diary of Olga Romanov:

Saturday. **6 April**. Had lessons. At 11 o'cl. we 5 went to the Manege with Papa for the Svodny Cossack regiment parade. Very nice. Papa and Alexei were wearing the Urals uniforms. Had breakfast with Mama and Nastenka.[98] In the afternoon broke ice with Papa. Sunny, warm, more than 15 degrees. Had tea with Papa and Mama. Had dinner with them and Count Grabbe. Everyone went to vsenoshnaya. So nice. Darling Mama also came and got tired.

---

[98] Anastasia Vasiliyevna Hendrikova, lady-in-waiting

From the 1913 diary of Olga Romanov:

Sunday. **7 April**. At 10 ½ went to obednya at the regimental church. After that there was a big breakfast. Dear AKSHV was there. [I] stared at his back from far away the entire time. Then [we] went out on the balcony. It was very bright, sunny, warm and windy. Went to see Derevenko, who finally returned from the hospital. Varvara Yuvchenko's son Evgeny, my godson, was there. So sweet. He is 4 months old. Mama rode in the park in an equipage. We walked around the garden breaking ice. Irina and [her] brothers had tea with us. After that we saw a cinematograph. Had dinner with Papa, Mama, Irina,

Feodor and Nikita. After that Prokudin-Gorsky[99] showed us interesting color photos. Went to bed after 11. Mama was tired.

1915 Letter from Maria to Nicholas II:

8 April. My sweet good Papa darling! Mama was terribly happy to receive the cross from you, and she is constantly wearing it today. She was lying down on the balcony for the first time today. Anastasia and I rode our bicycles for a bit around the house. The guard on duty today is not very interesting. In the morning it was 20 degrees in the sun. In the afternoon, I walked with Anastasia and Shura, and then went to our infirmary. Nikolaev has a toe abscess

---

[99] Famous contemporary pioneer in colour photography.

on his right foot, and they had to remove the nail, so now he has to stay in bed for a few days. [...] I am so happy for you, that you will see Aunt Olga. Do you remember when Tatiana Andreievna was here and asked for you to come over, back then you didn't think that you would be there so soon. Right now, I am sitting near Mama's bed, where she is staying, while Olga and Tatiana are reading. Alexei wanted to sleep in your spot today and told Mama that he wants to pretend that he is the husband. Yesterday he gorged on black crackers and in the evening, he was sent directly to Derevenko. Olga and Tatiana were in Petrograd today, Olga at the charities, and Tatiana at the committee and [she] took pleasure in dear Neidegart. After dinner I played kolorito with Mama. Now she is reading some English book. Yesterday Kozhevnikov and Rodionov and Kublitzky were at Anya's for tea. Before that they stopped by to bid farewell to Mama, as they were leaving that evening. They were wearing the same shirts as yours. It is so lonesome here without you. I kiss you affectionately, and squeeze you in hugs and love you. Your Kazanetz. Big regards to Kolya. May the Lord keep you. + [...]

From the 1913 diary of Tatiana Romanov:

HOLY WEEK. **9 April**. Tuesday. [...] [We] climbed up
the White Tower. Then broke ice. Had tea downstairs
with Papa, Mama, Aunt Ksenia and Uncle Sandro.[100]
Later went to church again, and Mama too. Had
dinner downstairs. Went to bed at 10 o'cl.

---

[100] Grand Duke Alexander Mikhailovich, husband of Grand Duchess Ksenia
Alexandrovna.

From 1916 diary of Alexei Romanov:

10 April. Got up at ½ 11. Exchanged Easter greetings with everyone. Mama was giving out eggs to everyone. Had breakfast with O., T., M. and A. In the evening rode around and visited Kolya. Went to bed early.

From the 1913 diary of Olga Romanov:

Thursday. **11 April**. At 9 o'clock received communion in the small chapel. A few regiment officers were there too. After that [we] rode with Nastenka. Wonderful weather. Had breakfast, tea and dinner with Papa and Mama. In the afternoon I stayed on the balcony and baked in the sun. Mama also was lying out there for a bit. She does not feel well. Her back aches a lot. There was a Reading of the 12 Scriptures upstairs. Towards the end, with great joy I unexpectedly saw dear AKSHV. [We] returned with lit candles.

1915 letter, Anastasia to Nicholas II:

12 April. My precious Papa! We just finished dinner, and Shvybzik[101] is getting terribly busy with Ortipo. This morning we went to church, as usual. Then had breakfast. Then Olga, Maria and Tatiana rode, the eldest steered themselves. Mama and Anya sat on the balcony. We then went to the local infirmary to [see] the wounded. There are more than a 100 of them there already, and one of Mama's Crimeans was there, black like an agate. Then we also went to the Siberian regiment infirmary, there were 50 lower ranks. This morning it was raining, but later it got wonderfully sunny and kind of humid. At 5 o'clock we went to Anya's, Shvedov, Zborovsky and Demenkov were there,

---

[101] Anastasia's pet dog.

it was very nice. We had tea in the dining room, and almost the entire time there played various games. Shvybzik was there of course. Viktor Erastovich[102] thinks that Shvybzik would make a very good diver. The lake in front of the entrance, there is almost no ice [on it], so pleasant. Olga is playing the piano. So tiresome that [we have] lessons tomorrow. I would like to ride my bicycle tomorrow. I am so embarrassed that my thoughts are so scattered. The "Garden of Eden" was almost entirely under water. It's so nice that you were able to visit everywhere, and the Peremyshel. Mama was terribly happy to get your telegram. Nagorny said that one cannot walk on the ice edges and that the ice is much softer but he could not break it, as he was taking a walk, I think. Mama is reading a letter from the soldiers, one of them is so awfully sweet, here it is: "To Her Imperial Majesty the Empress Alexandra Feodorovna. Dear Madame! Your Easter gifts transformed the soldiers! They were all filled with irrepressible fortitude and courage. Like the Saintly Apostles on the day when the Holy Spirit visited them [and] they spoke in foreign tongues, we too now express our joy though various events, only with subtle anticipation. Limitlessly loyal to Your

---

[102] Viktor Erastovich Zborovsky.

Imperial Majesty, the front position warrior of the 183rd Infantry of Pultunsky Regiment, who is always ready to give response." Sweet. Here is one more. I will rewrite it with the [original] mistakes. The letter from 1915, 5 April. "In the first line of my letter, I greet you my dear Mama your Imperial Majesty Empress Alexandra Feodorovna, regards from your little son Feodor Ivanovich I bow low to you and wish you good health from the Lord and from all us Christians wish you long life Received your package on 4 Apr. Received Feodor Ivanovich." There. Probably they will bring Anya here again, as she has been here every day. I will now squeeze [juice] from an orange and then have a lesson. I kiss you affectionately. Your faithful and loyal daughter. Shvybzik ANRPKZS-Nastasia. May God keep you. Regards to Nikolai Pavlovich and others.

From the 1918 diary of Nicholas II

13 April. Saturday. At 4 o'clock said goodbye to our dear children and climbed in to tarantasses[103]: I – with Yakovlev,[104] Alix- with Maria, Valya – with Botkin. Among our people the following went with us: Nyuta Demidova, Chemodurov and Sednev,[105] 9 marksmen and Calvary convoy (Red Army) of 10 men. The weather was cold with unpleasant wind, the road was

---

[103] A type of flat sleigh.
[104] Vasily Yakovlev, Commissar "Extraordinaire" who transferred Nicholas, Alexandra, and Maria from Tobolsk to Ekaterinburg .
[105] The imperial family's cook.

very bad, and awfully bumpy from the frozen tracks. Crossed Irtysh in rather deep water. Changed horses four times, making 130 versts the first day. Came to Ievlevo village to spend the night. Got settled in a large clean house; slept deeply on our cots.

From 1916 diary of Alexei Romanov:

14 April. Got up early. Studied and took a walk. Had breakfast with Papa, Mama, O., T., M., A., Aunt Ksenia and Sandro. In the afternoon took a walk and misbehaved. Had dinner at 6 o'cl. Was at Mama's in the evening. Went to bed early.

15 April. Got up early. Studied and took a walk. Had breakfast with Papa, Mama, O., T., M., A., and

Vilkitsky. In the afternoon took a walk and a ride. Papa, Mama and the sisters were at Aunt Mavra.[106] Took a ride. Was at Mama's for dinner. Went to bed early.

16 April. Studied and took a walk. Had breakfast with Papa, Mama, O., T., M., A., Uncle Georgiy, Count Fredericks and Dmitri Sheremetiev. In the afternoon took a walk and a ride in boats. Had dinner at 6 o'cl. Was at Mama's for dinner. Went to bed early.

---

[106] Grand Duchess Elizaveta Mavrikievna, wife of Grand Duke Konstantin Konstantinovich.

From the 1904 diary of Nicholas II:

17th April. Saturday. At 10 o'cl. left Petersburg with Misha (on duty). When [we] arrived at Tsarskoe Selo the sun peeked out and the weather got warmer. At 12 o'cl. on the square of the Grand Palace there was a parade of the 1st and 2nd sharpshooter battalions and the 6th Don battery. All the parts presented excellently.

From a 1918 letter, Alexandra to Olga
(Ekaterinburg to Tobolsk):

[**18(?) April**...] Your old mother is always with you in her thoughts, my dear Olga. The three of us are constantly talking about you and wonder what all of you are doing. The beginning of the trip was unpleasant and depressing; it was better after we got into the train. It's not clear how things will be there.

From the 1915 diary of Nicholas II:

19th April. Sunday. Today it was a very hot day—in the train cars the temp. reached 22°. Despite the heat [I] had to read and finish the paperwork which was brought by three couriers. During [the reading of] certain pages got up to stretch my legs.

From the 1904 diary of Nicholas II:

20th April. Tuesday. At one in the morning went on duck hunt near Gatchina and killed 2 grouses. Returned home at 5 o'cl. It rained the entire night. During the day as well, but was also quite warm. Alix had gone to the city to her warehouse and returned for tea. Engalychev had breakfast. Took a walk. Studied a lot in the evening.

From the 1914 diary of Nicholas II:

21st April. Monday. In the morning took a nice walk along the shore. The cold wind which was blowing these last few days stopped, and it was very warm in the sun. Before breakfast, received the commander of the 1st Siberian army Corporal Gen. Pleshkov and Knyazhevich. In the afternoon strenuously played some tennis. Had tea with the officers at home. Read before and after dinner.

From the 1904 diary of Nicholas II:

22nd April. Thursday. At one in the morning went to the same duck hunt, this time got lucky and killed five grouses. The night was wonderful. Returned home at 5 ¼. Slept until 9 ¾. There were three reports. Had breakfast alone together. Took a long walk. After tea I gifted Alix with a few things. Had dinner and spent the evening alone together.

Olga to Empress Alexandra: 23 April, 1917

"For suffering of others, you are full of anguish,

And no one's grief bypasses you.

Only to yourself are you relentless

Always merciless and forever cold!

But if your loving soul could see

Just once with someone else's eyes your sorrow –

Oh, how you would pity you.[107]

And how you would weep so sadly for yourself!"

To my beloved Mama

---

[107] Poem by Aleksei Konstantinovich Tolstoy, penned in 1859. Grand Duchess
Olga copied it down and dedicated it to her beloved mother, Empress
Alexandra Feodorovna, on 23 April, 1917.

From the 1914 diary of Nicholas II:

24th April. Thursday. The best day in terms of the weather. At 10 o'cl. went to Kurpati and returned home at 12 o'cl. Received the head of the City of Odessa, Pelikan. Around 3 o'cl. rode past the Farm to the Ai-Nikola meadow, where there was horse racing, cutting and fancy riding by the Crimeans. Everything was very nicely set up and went well. Were home by 5 o'cl. There were masses of onlookers, almost the entire Yalta. After tea, sat down to do paperwork and finished it by 10 ½ o'cl.

From a letter of Tatiana Romanov:

25 April, 1917. Tsarskoe Selo. [...] With sadness
and joy I remember the two wondrous days spent by
us last year, where you are now enjoying the delightful
beach. [...]

From the 1913 diary of Nicholas II:

26th April. Friday. In the morning received Benkendorf and Saltykov, read, took a walk; at 11 o'cl. received Kokovtsev and Gen. Markov, the new Min.[ister] St.-Secr. of the Finnish G.[rand] D.[uchy]. Sashka Vorontsov (on duty) had breakfast and dinner. Received the Kievan Exhibition Committee deputation. Rode bicycles with the daughters and canoed. At 6 o'cl. received Scheglovitov, Kasso and Dedulin. In the evening studied until 11 o'cl. At tea read aloud.

From the 1913 diary of Nicholas II:

27th April. Saturday. Completely summery day. At
11 o'cl. rode a horse to the square in front of the
palace for the church parade of the L.-Guards
Equestrian artillery. Olga and Alexei followed in a
carriage behind. The Parade was brilliant. Breakfast
ended early. Enlisted Oranovky into the suite. Took a
walk and canoed with the daughters for a long time.
At 6 1/2 went to vsenoshnaya. Sandro Leikhtenb. (on
duty) had dinner. Read. At 11 o'cl. went to Petersburg
to the equestrian-artillery meeting for supper.

From the 1915 diary of Nicholas II:

28th April. Tuesday. A cool clear day. In the morning took a half hour walk. In the afternoon walked with Olga, as the rest were riding horses. Boated on the pond with Alexei. At 6 o'cl. received Sazonov. At 7 1/2 went to Mama's and had dinner with Ksenia. Returned to Tsarskoe by 11 1/4.

From the 1916 diary of Nicholas II:

29th April. Friday. Today is 25 years since Otsu!
The report was not long. Reviewed the tent in the
garden. At 2 1/2 o'cl. headed to the turnpike via the
Bobruisky highway, where I walked through the village
Saltanovka and turned right through the woods and
the farm to the ponds, where I boarded a motor[car].
The weather was nice. Studied until dinner and the
evening wrote to Poincare.[108]

---

[108] Raymond Poincare, the French president.

From the 1913 diary of Olga Romanov:

Tuesday. **30 April**. Had lessons. Had breakfast with Papa, Mama, Aunt Ducky,[109] Uncle Kirill, [110] Uncle Boris and Dmitri. Mama and Alexei stayed in the study. In the afternoon we 4 walked around the park with Papa and Anya, Mama [rode] in a carriage. It was cold, but sunny. Then [we] canoed. It was just 1 degree. It snowed and hailed. Had dinner with Papa and Mama. Then Mama read "Notes by Empress Elizaveta." Then Papa went off to read, and we worked until 10 o'cl.

---

[109] Grand Duchess Viktoria Feodorovna.
[110] Grand Duke Kirill Vladimirovich.

MAY

From the 1918 diary of Nicholas II:

1 May. Tuesday. We were overjoyed by the letters received from Tobolsk; I got one from Tatiana. We read each other's letters all morning. The weather was wonderful, warm. The guard was changed at noon, from the ranks of the same special frontier team— Russians and Latvians. The head—a presentable young man. Today they told us through Botkin that we are only allowed to walk one hour per day; and to the question why? The acting commandant replied "so that it is similar to a prisoner schedule." Food arrived on time. They bought us a samovar—at least we won't be dependent on the guards now. In the evening had four beziques during the game.

111

2 May. Wednesday. The application of the "prisoner" schedule continued and expressed itself in that an old

---

[111] Actual photo of the inside of Ipatiev house.

housepainter had painted over all our windows in all the rooms with lime. It started to seem like fog beyond the windows. Went to take a walk at 3 ½ and at 4.10 they chased us inside. There was not one extra soldier in the garden. The head guard did not speak to us since all this time one of the commissars was in the garden watching us, him and the guard! The weather was very nice, but the rooms got gloomy. Only the dining room benefitted because they took down the rug outside the window! Sednev has a cold with fever.

3 May. Thursday. The day was grey but warm. One could feel the dampness in the rooms especially our two; the air entering the window vent was warmer than inside. I taught Maria to play trick-track.

Sednev's fever is less, but he stayed in bed all day. Walked for exactly an hour. The guard order significantly increased, there were no more loiterers in the garden with us. During the day we got coffee, Easter eggs and chocolate from Ella in Perm. We lost electricity in the dining room, had supper with two candles in jars. In the hall, not everything had electricity either. Took a bath after Maria at 7 ½ o'cl.

1918 Letter from Olga to Ekaterinburg:

Saturday, 6 o'clock, **4th May.** We learned through a telegram from Matv.[eyev] that everything is fine. Oh my God, how are you? It is horrible not to be together and to know nothing about you, because what we are told generally is not always the truth. [...] May God protect you. O.

5 May [continued]. ХРИСТОС ВОСКРЕСЕ! [CHRIST HAS RISEN!] Dear beloved ones. We would love so much to know how you celebrated your Easter. Dear Mama, when will we finally be together? May God look after you. The midnight mass and the service afterwards were well done. It was beautiful and intimate. We put on all the side lights, except for the chandelier and there was enough light. The Little One[112] slept during the service and did not participate in the Easter supper and did not even notice that we moved him to his bedroom.

---

[112] Alexei.

Today at 10:30 we gave Easter greetings to everyone and offered eggs. Everyone thanked us, in fact the nuns sang well as a whole, but the Easter hymns were dreadful, in the style of popular dances and at top speed. The candles were beautiful, with the golden stripes and it was for you that we lit them, in turns during the Easter mass, as well as Zina's candle. There are a lot of eggs, kuliches[113] and paskas[114], etc. Mama, my little soul, how are things with you? I feel sad—when I think about you—why do we have everything and you, what do you have? Dear and beloved Mama, how I would love to see you and kiss you!!

---

[113] Easter bread.
[114] Easter cake.

At this moment Klavd[ia] Mikh.[ailovna],[115] Nastenka and the general are with the Little One. Rostovtsov sends his greeting by telegram as well as Kupytch, who writes about Voronezh and remembers the year 1915. We hear the sound of bells all the time. The weather is bad.[116]

From the 1915 diary of Nicholas II:

6th May. Wednesday. Pouring rain during the night, it got cooler and the day remained overcast. Before the morning tea, the suite and the people wished me a happy birthday. At 10 o'cl. went to [hear] a report, then to obednya. Had breakfast with everyone in the tent behind Nikolasha's train. Received Engalychev

---

[115] Klavdia Mikhailovna Bitner.
[116] Letter ends here abruptly, so it is probable that a page is missing.

with a report. Took a walk around half the woods. Read and responded to telegrams. After dinner played some dominoes.

From the 1915 diary of Tatiana Romanov:

Thursday, **7 May**. [...] Drove with Mama to the infirmary. Officer Lignasevich of the 150th Taman Regiment had surgery. Very seriously wounded. [They] made an incision in the right leg [and] took out the bullet. Then dressings [...] [They] brought in three more officers. Saw everyone of course. Breakfast with Mama 5. Said goodbye to Karangozov and Gordinsky. At 2 o'clock there was a big meeting at the Grand

Palace. Mama was there too. Took photographs.
Went to [see] the wounded. Had tea with Mama. At 7
o'clock said goodbye to Alexei and the sisters and
departed. Had dinner on the train with Isa, Resin,
Zolotarev and two engineers.

Friday, **8 May**. At 9 o'clock in the morning arrived in
Vitebsk. Went to the cathedral, where there was a
short moleben. Then went to infirmaries. Had
breakfast on the train. Wonderful weather. Warm,
and the greenery blossomed everywhere. Had
breakfast on the train. At 3 o'clock drove to Mama's
Red Cross warehouse. Then to three infirmaries. After
that to have tea at the governor's house. When we

arrived at the station, walked around the hospital train. At 7 o'clock left. Had dinner like yesterday and went to bed early.

From the 1913 diary of Olga Romanov:

Thursday. **9 May**. From 9 o'cl. 15 min. until 10 o'cl. [I] sat on the balcony with T and baked in the sun. After that had lessons. Had breakfast with Mama and Aunt Olga. In the afternoon we 4 and Aunt Olga went riding. We rode by the church, the barracks and the Assembly ([I] hoped to see my dear) and got lucky. AKSHV and a bunch of other officers were on the balcony. So nice. At about 3 ½ met N.P. (it's his name day today) at Znamenie and went to Mama's. Sat on the balcony and had tea cozily. Had dinner with Mama and spent the evening with her and Anya. Papa sent a lovely lilac bouquet and a letter to Mama from [Germany?]. He sent a telegram from Berlin.

From 1916 diary of Alexei Romanov:

10 May. At 10 o'cl. ¼ went to the review. We saw the Russian soldiers and 3 regiments of the Serbian ones. When we returned from the parade, Papa and I saw the small museum. Had breakfast with Mama. 2 o'cl. 45 m. went to see the iodine producing factory. Then went to see the clinic for healing mud baths, in two places on the shore of the Black Sea. Had dinner with Mama on the train.

From the 1915 letter of Tatiana Romanov:

11 May. Papa darling. Forgive me that I did not write for so long, but somehow there was never enough time. Today Mama, Olga and I went to obednya at the grotto church of our infirmary, and then changed dressings of the officers and lower ranks. We now have many new officers. Yesterday evening we had dinner with Mama earlier and at 8 o'clock went to Anya's. Alexei was there too and remained until 9. Ravtopulo[117] arrived there, the Swedes, Yusik Zolotarev and of course Demenkov. It was very nice

---

[117] Boris Ravtopulo- an officer in the Yerevan regiment.

and merry. And yesterday afternoon we were at Tatiana's. Poor thing, she was just starting to recover, and when she was standing on crutches she suddenly lost her balance and fell, of course on the injured leg, and again tore all the ligaments that have just started to heal. Her children were terribly nice, and we romped around with them a lot. The other day the new commander, your Yerevanetz, presented himself to Mama. He is not very big and has cavalry-like legs. Vitebsk was very good. Olga probably wrote to You about everything we did there, but I wanted to tell you that it was awfully nice. As we approached the governor's house, a band was playing, which met us with a Cavalry march[118] instead of Uhlan. We laughed a lot—so sweet. Well, goodbye. Papa darling, the man will leave now, and I am afraid that the letter to be too late. May God keep You. I kiss You firmly and gently, as much as I love [you], your VOZNESENETZ.

---

[118] In the XIX century, military music in Russia became very diverse, and each regiment had its own march, making it able to determine which regiment was approaching by the music that was played. In 1826, at the request of his wife, Tsar Nicholas I ordered that the March for the Cavalry Guards was to be a melody from the opera *La Dame Blanche* by French composer Francois-Adrien Boileau. Knowing that Tatiana was approaching, the band should have played the march belonging to the Uhlan regiment.

From the 1918 diary of Nicholas II:

12 May. Saturday. Everyone slept well, except Alexei, who was moved to his own room yesterday. He continues to have terrible pains, which alleviate periodically. The weather was completely appropriate for our mood, wet snow with 3° of warmth. We conducted talks though Evg.[eniy] S.[ergeievich] with the head of the Regional Soviet about allowing m-r Gilliard to join us. The children unpacked some of their things after an unbelievably long search of them in the commandant's room. Walked for about 20 minutes.

13 May. Sunday. Slept wonderfully, except Alexei. His pains persist, but with long breaks. He stayed in bed in our room. There was no [religious] service. The weather was the same, snow on the roofs. As in all the recent days, V.N. Derevenko came to examine Alexei; today a dark gentleman was accompanying him, who we thought was a doctor. After a short walk we entered the barn where our large baggage was dropped off with commandant Avdeyev[119]. The search of some unopened chests continued. Started to read the works of Saltykov [Shedrin] from the bookcase of the owner of the house. In the evening played bezique.

---

[119] Alexander Avdeyev, commandant of the Ipatiev House before Yakov Yurovsky.

From the 1896 diary of Tsar Nicholas II:

14th May. Tuesday. Grand, solemn, but difficult day, in the moral sense, for Alix, Mama and me. From 8 o'cl. in the morning were on our feet; and our procession moved only at 1/2 of 10. Fortunately, the weather was marvelous; the Red Porch presented a radiant appearance. All this happened in the Uspensky [Assumption] Cathedral, though it seems like a real dream, but will not forget for the rest of my life!!! Returned to our [rooms] at half past two. At 3 o'clock walked in the same procession once again, to Granovitaya Chamber for a meal. At 4 o'clock it all ended quite well; with a soul full of gratitude to God, later I was quite rested. Dined at Mama's, who fortunately survived this long ordeal excellently. At 9 o'cl. we walked to the upper balcony, where Alix lit the electric illumination on the Ivan the Great [Bell], and then the towers and walls of the Kremlin were lit sequentially, as well as the opposite embankment and Zamoskvorechye. [We] went to bed early.

From the 1918 diary of Nicholas II:

15 May. Tuesday. Today is a month since our arrival here. Alexei feels the same—only the restful breaks are longer. The weather was hot, stuffy, but cool inside. Had dinner at 2 o'clock. Walked and sat in the garden an hour and 1/4. Alix cut my hair successfully.

120

From the 1916 diary of Tatiana Romanov:

Monday, **16 May**. In the morning arrived in Evpatoria[121]. Went to the cathedral for moleben, from there to a mosque, then to the Karaite temple. Went to Mama's sanatorium. Rita was there, a lot of the wounded and many of ours. Examined everything, then stopped by a small infirmary. Breakfast on the train. In the afternoon went to Anya's dacha. Rita was there too. Sat on a marvelous beach near the sea, hunted for seashells. Had tea on her balcony. Returned at 6 o'clock. All our wounded were at the train station. Sat at home. Had dinner with everyone. At 9 o'clock walked with Papa along the Sarabuz station. Left Anya there. Later sat with Mama. – Terribly sad to leave the Crimea, the sea, the sailors and the ships!

---

[120] Actual photograph from 16 May, 1916.
[121] A city in the Crimea.

From the 1913 diary of Olga Romanov:

Minin on the Volga River. Friday. **17 May.** At 10 o'cl. [we] arrived in Nizhny Novgorod. The honor guard from the 37th Ekaterinburg regiment was there. From there we went to the Spaso-Preobazhensky Cathedral. Troops were lined up along the streets. Schools and gymnasiums were there too. After molebna Mama and Alexei went to the palace. We went down to Minin's[122] grave, where a litia[123] was held. Then we walked in a procession to the site of the future monument for

---

[122] Kuzma Minin was a Russian merchant who fought against the Polish invasion.
[123] A service held after liturgy or vespers to commemorate departed family members.

Prince Pozharsky and Prince Minin. There was ceremonial marching. Went back to the palace and had breakfast. Mama and we 4 received the Matushka[124] and the ladies. Papa received the local leaders, then he went to visit the new bank. We stayed with Mama—she was very tired of course. May God grant her strength. At 4 ½ went to have tea with [the local] nobility. There were masses of people. I sat with Kvoshinsky's sister—she is very sweet. Then [we] went to the pier— [it was] far. The owners of the Volga shipbuilding factories with their families greeted us there, toasted to everyone's health, shouted "Hurrah," etc. Our steamer is awfully cozy. My cabin is portside, near Mama's cabin (Gulyga, Zborovoy, the good constable Shapkin). Cool, overcast. A big dinner was served in the "Tsar Mikhail Feodorovich"[125] dining hall. We 2 and Papa went to dinner. Appealing, big dining hall. A bit after 10 o'cl. we sailed off. Mama's heart No. 3—May God bless [her].

---

[124] The Mother Superior, literally translated as "Little Mother."
[125] The first Romanov tsar, elected in 1613.

Letter from Maria to Z.S. Tolstaya.

Ekaterinburg, 4/**17 May, 1918.** Christ Has Risen.
My dear Z., Good wishes to you for this bright holiday.
I apologize for [writing] so late, but we departed right
before the holidays. It was very unexpected for us.
Alexei happened to be sick, so the sisters had to stay
with him. They are supposed to arrive here soon. Tell
Rita that not that long ago we saw the little Sedusha.
Today is three weeks since we left Tobolsk. It is so sad
to be without the others, especially now during the
holidays. We have settled in nicely here. The house is
small but clean, shame that it's right in the city so the
garden is rather small. When the others arrive, not
sure how we will settle, there are not that many rooms.
I live with Papa and Mama in one, where we spend
almost the entire day. Just now we went out into the
garden, the weather is gray and it is raining. On the

way, the weather was wonderful. We rode horses for 260 versts until Tyumen. The roads were awful, we were jolted terribly. The paper with which our things were wrapped rubbed out in places. Tobacco fell out of the cigarettes. But strangely no glass broke. We took the medicines with us and arrived safely. Rode for two days, stayed the nights in a village. Took horses across the Irtysh, and walked across the Tura on foot and a few sazhens[126] to the banks—in a ferry. Mama withstood the journey surprisingly well, but now of course feels tired and has a headache almost daily. Doctor Botkin came with us, the poor man had kidney colic on the way, he was suffering a lot. We stopped in a village and they put him to bed there, he rested for two hours and continued with us. Luckily the pains did not happen again. And how are you all? The sisters wrote to you, that we got news from you. If you want to write to me, my address is: Ekaterinburg, the Regional Executive Committee. To the Chairman, to be given to me. Have you had any news from Tili[127]? Regards to all yours and Nik. Dm. I kiss you, Rita, and the children affectionately. I wish you all the best. May the Lord keep you. It was terribly sad that

---

[126] A sazhen is a unit of measurement about seven feet.
[127] Their nickname for Lili Dehn.

we were not able to go to the cathedral even once and venerate the relics of St. Ioann of Tobolsk.

From the 1913 diary of Olga Romanov:

Same—along the Kama River. Saturday. **18 May.** We proceeded along until 9 o'cl. 45 min. Now we stopped on the pier. It is very cold and windy. [We] walked on the deck, sat, went on the deck-bridge, etc., had breakfast with Papa and everyone in the afternoon. Mama went upstairs to lie down in the cabin. The wind subsided by evening, it was sunny all day. Mama has a headache, her heart aches. Beautiful surroundings—masses of people. Went to bed at 11 o'cl. We were learning to curtsy in Mama's cabin. It was very funny.

From the 1913 diary of Maria Romanov:

19 May Sunday. In the morning there was obednya and molebna at the Ipatiev monastery.[128] 5 with Mama and Papa. At breakfast sat with Botkin and Dedulin. In the afternoon we 5 with Papa and Mama saw Tsar Mikhail Feodorovich's museum. Then there was tea with the Nobility. Had dinner with Anastasia, Alexei, Nilov[129] and Sablin.

---

[128] Ipatiev Monastery in Kostroma was the asylum of the sixteen-year-old first Romanov tsar and his mother before he was elected.
[129] General-Adjutant Admiral Konstantin Dmitrievich Nilov was the tsar's flag captain and one of his friends.

Letter from Tatiana to Nicholas II:

20 May 1916. Today it is 20 [degrees] in the sun, but cold in the shade. We will go to the infirmary, [our] lessons start. All our rooms were cleaned, they seem so big after the cozy train. Iedigarov told us many interesting things about how they are fighting over there, about the regiment and a lot of things in general. Well, good-bye, Papa darling. May God bless You. I kiss you both firmly and gently, my dears. Your Voznesenetz.

From the 1913 diary of Olga Romanov:

Tuesday, **21 May.** On the train to Yaroslavl, 12 o'cl. 20 min. in the morning. Arrived here at 9 o'cl. [It is] very warm but windy. An honor guard of the 181st Ostrolensky regiment met us at the pier. Rashpil and AKSHV were there. Yuzik was [on guard] by the Uspensky Cathedral. From there we went to the Church of Ioann the Baptist, a very interesting old church. Before that we went to the [illeg] Church (AKSHV), were the Icon of the Savior is kept (the one that saved the city from the plague). Then we visited

the Spassky Monastery, were we saw the vestry and
the living quarters of Mikhail Feodorovich, were he
stayed for 26 days after the coronation. From there we
went to the Ilyinsky church, and again looked at the
antiques. Returned after 1 o'clock, had breakfast with
masses of people in the Tsar Mikhail Feodorovich
dining hall. Mama and Al[exei] returned from the
cathedral. After 3 o'cl. we 4 and Papa went to the
consecration ceremony of an orphanage
commemorating the 300th anniversary. From there we
went to the Exhibit of Yaroslavl Province's
manufacturing. Masses of gifts, [we] got very tired, [it
was] very long and boring, also very hot. At 5 o'cl. 15
min. [we] went to the Tolgsky Monastery. Very
beautiful (AKSHV). Mama and Al[exei] came too.
Moleben, vestry. Returned and had dinner in the
middle of the river, a little farther. Heavy rain,
thunderstorm, gusts. Returned at 9 o'cl. At 10 o'cl.
we went to the Assembly of the Nobility with Papa and
Mama. Zbruyevs, Sobinov, the quartet, N.P. performed
very well. It was hot, had tea. The gymnasium
students sang. At 12 o'cl. we were [back] on the train.
The good sweet AKSHV was there. I was terribly
happy to see him. Poor Mama got very tired. Heart
No. 3, aches. May the Lord save her.

From the 1913 diary of Maria Romanov:

22 May. Arrived in Rostov. We 5 with Papa went to the Uspensky Cathedral, then walked along the Kra[illeg] from there to the White Chamber and Princely Tower. On the way looked at churches. At breakfast sat with Count Benkendorf and Mosolov. In the afternoon we went to the Pokrovsky Monastery and church of St. Ioann. Had tea 5 with Papa and the suite. Went to vsenoshnaya at the Christ's Resurrection church. At dinner sat with Benkendorf and Mosolov.

From the 1916 diary of Tatiana Romanov:

Monday, **23 May.** In the morning, went for a walk with Anastasia and Trina, from 9 to 10 o'clock. Then to Znamenie and to the infirmary. Olga rides with me, Mama too, a little. Surgery on a soldier, excised the leg bone. Handed the instruments. Bandaged Natarov. Sat on the balcony with Pavlov, Mitya and Borya[130] came [over]. Stayed with them. Breakfast 4 with Mama on the balcony. Had tea and dinner there. Had a lesson. Then rode "Kopriko." It was wonderful. Around Pavlovsk. After tea [had a] lesson. Then rode with Nastenka and the sisters. After dinner we all

---

[130] Possibly Ravtopulo

went to the infirmary. Picked up Bibi on the way. There we cleaned the instruments and sewed compresses until 11:45. Borya and Mitya were there, too.

From the 1913 diary of Olga Romanov:

Friday. **24 May.** Moscow. At 10 o'cl. [we] arrived at the Troitze-Sergeyevsky Monastery. Went to obednya, reveled the relics, had tea with the Metropolitan. Wonderful weather (Zborovsky, Beliy and Serbakov). At 3 ½ arrived in Moscow. Stopped by different houses. We 4 with Aunt Ella,[131] Papa, the relatives,

---

[131] Grand Duchess Elizaveta Feodorovna, widow of Grand Duke Sergei Alexandrovich. Aunt-by-marriage to the tsar and sister to the empress.

the Imperial suite [were] on horseback. A hundred Guards at the front. Dear AKSHV smiled across the crowd. N.P., the good B.-B., Count Nirod were [all] there. Very nice in general. The Sumsky regimental squadron followed [us] in the back. Obednya or Litia, not sure, was held at the Arkhangelsk Cathedral. Papa lit the oil burner under the tomb of the tsars, then walked back. Had tea with Papa, Mama, Aunt Olga and Aunt Ksenia. Poor Mama was very tired. Temperature 37.2 in the morning, heart 2.5. Had dinner with Papa and Aunt Ksenia. Mama was in bed. May the Lord save her. Gr[igori] Ye[fimovich][132] was standing outside the cathedral.

---

[132] Grigori Yefimovich Rasputin.

From the 1916 diary of Maria Romanov:

25 May. Went to obednya with Mama. Had breakfast with same on the balcony. Went to your infirmary with A. Rode 4 with Nastenka. Had tea 4 on the balcony with Mama, Aunt Olga, Aunt Mavra, and Aunt Miechen.[133] Drove 4 with Mama to Anya's house, were we saw Grigori and Munika. Had dinner 4 with Mama. Went to the sisters' infirmary, put together a puzzle with Grekova, the Countess, Natarovich, Nikiforov, Karankozov and the Doctor.

---

[133] Grand Duchess Maria Pavlovna "the Elder," widow of Grand Duke Vladimir Alexandrovich.

From the 1913 diary of Olga Romanov:

Sunday. **26 May.** At 11 o'cl. we 4 and Papa went to the Novospassky Monastery for obednya. Alexei came towards the end, for litia. [We] went to see the ancestor tombs downstairs. Gr[igori] Yef[imovich] was there. Had breakfast at Aunt Ella's with Papa and Aunt Olga. Came back and in a ¼ hour went to the municipal council. Had tea there and accepted gifts. From a window watched the boys perform gymnastics. Had tea with Papa, Mama and Aunt Ella. After that S.I. came over with her sister and nephew. Had dinner with Papa and mama and at 10 o'cl. went to the Assembly of the Nobility. AKSHV was there. The polonaise started. I walked in with Troyanov. It was very beautiful. I danced a lot. Once with N.P. and once with dear Otar Purtzeladze. Was very happy to see the Yerevansky regiment officers, unexpectedly B.-B. and Count Nirod were there. Saw all my friends. During a quadrille saw AKSHV's sweet smiling face from far away. Very, very nice. Towards the end I just wanted to leave, had a peculiar feeling for some reason. Mama left earlier. We came back at 12 ½. Wonderful warm weather. Thank you, God for everything. Mama is tired.

Anastasia to Nicholas II:

27 May, 1916. T.S. My dear Papa Darling! I will soon send you the pictures that I took in Mogilev and Sevastopol, if you want them! Yesterday when I was riding around, long distance passenger train passed by

and suddenly I saw through the window a protective e,
a red beshmet and papakha, and further in the
window a gray cherkesska and I thought I recognized
Count Grabbe and his Cossack, and then during the
day we ran into Voikov, he was riding in a motor. Tell
Alexei that I plan to write to him, but never have time.
We now pick flowers; the lilac is here already but not
that much of it. The weather is not great, it rains daily
nevertheless we still have breakfast and tea on the
balcony. Right now, I don't have a lesson and
therefore I can write. Have you heard anything about
the 1st Hundred! The probably have enough to do now
and are rather happy. Sometimes a Hundred comes
by here for practice and returns with zurna, so of
course we eyeball [them] and yesterday they passed
and I watched. It's a shame there are too many
bushes so they can't see us well, but the important
thing of course is that we can see them. We will now
accompany the sisters to their infirmary and ride back
for our lessons. Everyone gives you a big kiss and
Alexei too. Your loving loyal and faithful little
Kaspiyitz. May God keep you!

Letter from Nicholas II to Tatiana:

Stavka **28 May, 1916**. Dearest Tatiana.

Congratulations on your birthday and I wish you good health and all the best. I regret that I cannot spend time with you on this day! Thank you very much for writing the letters, which give me great pleasure. Alexei and I often remember our trip and especially Sevastopol! It was so nice to be there among the sailors! Alexei named this one place here with soft sand on the banks of the Dnieper— "Evpatoria" and [he] loves it. Every other day we ride on the river in motor boats and dinghies. Tell Olga that I chose four photographs and [am] returning the rest and [I] thank her. How did you like Zhylik's letter; he was afraid to send it, but I insisted you get it. These days it is hot and the weather is wonderful and it is during this time that different ministers are pestering me! Thank God that things are going well for us in the south-west, now the total number of prisoners has reached 77,000 men. Grandmama will probably see a lot, because they all gather in Kiev first. I'm glad that you go [horseback] riding, but why not with the sisters? Today the miraculous icon of Our Lady of Vladimir arrived from Moscow and at 5 o'cl. they will solemnly take [it] to our church. Well, I've got to finish now. I embrace you and the sisters. May Christ be with you. + Your Papa.

1916 Letter from Maria to Nicholas II:

29 May. [At] the Feodorovsky Cathedral Imperial infirmary for the wounded. My dear Papa! I don't think I ever wrote to you on this paper before. Today it was hot here, but now [it is] not that [hot], as it rained a little. In the morning we went to obednya and had breakfast on the balcony, also had tea with Zizi.[134] She is leaving to her village tomorrow. I am all bitten up by some nasty beast, and therefore my entire body itches. It is extremely unpleasant, especially in public, when one has to scratch. These days we go to the sisters' infirmary almost every evening. They clean the

---

[134] Elizaveta Naryshkina, mistress of the robes.

instruments and prepare materials for the next day. Anastasia plays table croquet with the wounded, while I play bloshki or put together a puzzle. This afternoon we rode around, and then went to our infirmary. Almost all the wounded are lying in the tent, only the heavily [wounded] ones are not allowed. Those who are able, walk to Catherine Park and sail around the lake in row boats. They really enjoy this and always ask the nurses to go with them. We go to our infirmary every day too, this is much better than the Grand Palace with Nurse Lyubushina. She of course noted that we got tan and all the nurses too. The other day we went to Children's Island[135] with Poupse's[136] sister, and she weeded with us. There is so much decayed grass among the lilies of the valley that they are not growing well. We cleaned half, and will finish the other half in one of the next couple of days. I kiss you and Alexei very affectionately. May God keep you. + Your Kazanetz.

---

[135] Island in Alexander Park, where there was a playhouse that had been built in 1830 for the children of Tsar Nicholas I.
[136] Presumably a nickname for one of the suite or officers. Literally means "baby doll."

From the 1913 diary of Olga Romanov:

Thursday, **30 May.** Had lessons: religion and German. Maria has a sore throat and was moved into a separate room. Temperature 36.7, 38.8, 38.4, 38.1. Had breakfast and tea with Papa and Mama. Had dinner with them and Aunt Mavra. Mama slept well but was tired of course. In the afternoon sat on the balcony with Mama, then—with Nastasia and Derevenko. Pretty warm, wonderful lilac. Had a music lesson. Alexei's temperature 38.2, also has a sore throat.

Letter from Anastasia to Nicholas II:

31 May 1916. Tsarskoe Selo. We are having lessons now, but as of tomorrow we will still have lessons but not during the day anymore, and this will be very pleasant. These days Maria and I swing on giant steps[137] a lot. We are almost never nauseous (although we fell a bunch of times already, but so far have not hurt ourselves). We went riding now as there is no lesson and now we are waiting for Mama and the sisters [to return] from the infirmary. We go there evenings and I play croquet which is sitting on a table. It is very small, but it is really fun to play. I play with 3 officers the entire evening until they send me to bed, although most of the time I go without an invitation.

---

[137] A swing-like game.

Now I must finish writing as it is time for frishtyk[138] on the balcony. Today it is windy but sunny and warm. I listen to your and Alexei's letters with great appetite during zakuski[139] or breakfast. I apologize that I am using different ink, but I am writing in mama's room. Well now! I give awfully big kisses to your sweet little cheeks and hands, and Alexei. May God keep you. Your loving loyal and faithful 14-year-old Kaspiyitz.

---

[138] Type of appetisers (German)
[139] Appetisers (Russian)

JUNE

From the 1913 diary of Olga Romanov:

Saturday. **1 June.** Had religion and German lessons. Cold and rainy. At 10 o'cl. had breakfast with Mama, Count Fredericks and Silaev. It was nice to hear about the regiment. In the afternoon tried on my uniform, and then rode in an equipage with the Uhlan.[140] I

---

[140] Reference to Tatiana and her regiment.

steered [it] myself. Papa and breakfast with the Hussars. Had tea with him and Mama. Had dinner with them and Silaev. Smoked afterwards. Before vsenoshnaya saw Gr[igori] Yef[imovich]. It was so nice in church, everything was green. Maria is feeling better, she is up. Alexei is too. Mama is tired.

From the 1913 diary of Maria Romanov:

2 June. Sunday. 5 went with Papa to a parade of the Izmailovsky Regiment and the Northern Battalion. Had breakfast 5 with Aunt Mavra and Mama on the sofa. In the afternoon 4 went in a motor with Anya to

Aunt Olga's in Peterhof. Had tea, took a walk. Played and had dinner. There were: Shvedov, Yuzik, Skvortzov, Zborovsky, Rodionov, Klyucharev, Kulikovsky, Aunt Ksenia with Irina, Andrusha and Feodor[141] and Anya and Semyonov. Returned home.

From the 1913 diary of Olga Romanov:

Tuesday. **3 June.** Peterhof. Got up late due to Bekker. Had breakfast with Papa, Mama and

---

[141] Prince Andrei Alexandrovich and Prince Feodor Alexandrovich, sons of Grand Duchess Ksenia Alexandrovna.

Bagration. At 2 o'cl. 10 min. went to Znamenie, and then to the [train] station. At 3 ½ arrived in Peterhof. Chilly, rather windy. Had tea with Papa and Mama, had dinner with them and Aunt Olga. Went to bed late. Papa read to us. Mama is well, thank God. I am lodging in 2 rooms upstairs.

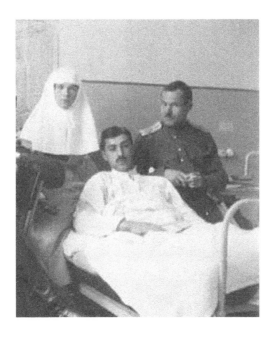

From the 1916 diary of Olga Romanov:

Saturday, **4th June.** Viktor Erastovich was wounded. Skvortsov too, but lightly, and 7 Cossacks. 1 was killed. Shurik is ill with typhus. To Znamenie and to the infirmary with Mama. Mitya and Borya came before 1 o'clock. Did all as usual. Raining and cold. Anya and Emma Fredericks with her father had breakfast again. During the day rode with Mama in 2 equipages. [We] were cold and wet. Saw Mitya from the Silayevs' window.

From the 1918 diary of Nicholas II:

5 June. Tuesday. Dear Anastasia turned 17 already. Great heat outside and inside. Continued reading III volume of Saltykov—engaging and intelligent.

The entire family walked before tea. Since yesterday Kharitonov[142] has been cooking our food, they bring provisions every two days. The daughters are learning to cook from him and are kneading dough in the evenings, and baking the bread in the mornings. Not bad!

---

[142] Ivan Mikhailovich Kharitonov, cook to the imperial family in exile.

From the 1913 diary of Maria Romanov:

6 June. Thursday. The dentist was here in the morning. Had breakfast 5 [with] Papa, Mama, Aunt Ksenia, Uncle Sandro and their children. Went to Aunt Olga's had tea there and played. [There] were: Shvedov, Yuzik, Skvortzov, Zborovsky, Kulikovsky and Aunt Ksenia with 4 strannitzy.[143] Had dinner with Anastasia and Alexei.

---

[143] Holy women.

From the 1913 diary of Olga Romanov:

Friday. **7 June.** At 11 o'cl. we went in motors to see Tatiana[144] in Strelna. Played with her son Teymuraz for a long time. From there we went to see the Countess Hendrikova.[145] Raining and 4 degrees, windy, foul. Had breakfast with Papa, Mama, Aunt Olga, Uncle Nik.[146] and Dmitri. In the afternoon [we] stayed home, read, played the piano. Mama and Papa went to visit Aunt Mops. After they returned we had tea together. Had dinner with Mama. Papa went to [see] the Cavalry Grenadier regiment. Aunt Ksenia's 3 boys played with Alexei.

---

[144] Princess Tatiana Konstaninovna.
[145] "Nastenka" Hendrikova's mother.
[146] Grand Duke Nikolai Mikhailovich.

From the 1913 diary of Tatiana Romanov:

8 June. Monday... Stayed in the garden for a little while, then went inside the house to have tea. Our Yerevantzy[147] friends came over there [several names listed]. We rested with them for about 25 min. Then returned alone. Had tea all together as usual. [I] was very happy to see the Yerevantzy. Went to vsenoshnaya. Had dinner 4 with Papa and Mama. At 10 o'cl. went to bed.

---

[147] From Yerevan.

Letter from Anastasia to Nicholas II:

9 June 1916. My dear Papa Darling. We just played ping pong with Maria and were bustling around and yelling so incredibly much that now my hands are shaking like someone with a head injury. I think that in a few days they will bring Viktor Erastovich to our infirmary, he requested for another coronet from the Tekinsky Regiment to come with him, they will bring them from Poltava. Of course, this is pleasant. We are now moving to a nearby infirmary, the one that looks out on to the Convoy gathering and the Sobor. We will have an infirmary there now, so very cozy. Maria and I went there a few times to look, and we were satisfied. Today Mama, Olga and Tatiana are going to the city for the Executive Committee, and I don't envy them, while

Maria and I are staying here. We keep swinging in the hammock. Well, when Vera and Georgiy[148] were here, they had breakfast [here] with their mother. So we picked them up and swung them, Vera was really happy, while Georgi kept getting scared, and then Vera and Georgiy started to fight, and we were instigating them a little against each other and laughing. It will probably start raining now, but of course I am not afraid of this as I am a brave little soldier. Well here it comes, congratulations!!! I wrote all the news and anything interesting, and the rest is the usual. Well, I will end my silly message now, masses of kisses to you and Alexei. May Christ be with you. Regards to all of yours. Miss [you]. Your loving loyal and faithful little Kaspiyitz. All the sisters kiss you.

---

[148] Princess Vera Konstantinovna and Prince Georgiy Konstantinovich, the youngest children of Grand Duke Konstantin Konstantinovich.

From the 1917 diary of Nicholas II:

10th June. Saturday. During the night and during the day until 3 o'cl. it continued to be swelteringly hot and muggy. Took a long walk in the morning. Had breakfast like yesterday, in the children's dining room. During the day worked in the same spot. A rain storm passed in the distance, there were a few drops of rain. Fortunately, it got cooler. At 6 1/2 went to vsenoshnaya. In the evening, around 11 o'cl. we heard a shot from the garden, after a ¼ hour the chief guard asked [permission] to come in and explained that a guard did shoot, as he thought he saw a red light signal from one of the children's bedroom windows. Having checked the location of the electric light and seeing the movement of Anastasia's head, [who was] sitting by the window, one of the unter-of.[ficers] who came in with him, realized what happened and they left, having apologized.

From the 1913 diary of Maria Romanov:

11 June. Tuesday. In the morning 4 with Nastenka and Trina went to [illeg] and Aunt Olga. At breakfast sat with Sangovich and Polushkin. In the afternoon took a walk on the "patio" with Papa, Aunt Olga, the ladies and officers. Had tea with Loya. Had dinner with Mama.

From the 1913 diary of Olga Romanov:

Wednesday. **12 June.** At 9 ½ we 4 with Nastenka, Trina and Kozhevnikov went ashore in a motorboat. There we met Aunt Olga, Knyazevich, Semyonov, and Tulupov on the rocks. We sat there, it rained, Semyonov read stories by Teffi to us. Returned by 11 o'cl. The officers of all the ships were invited to breakfast as usual. In the afternoon [we] went ashore with Papa, Aunt Olga, etc., near the telegraph. From there [we] walked to the village. Then we stretched out on the grass in the sun by the church. So nice and warm. Returned to where Alexei was playing with the boys. Maria and Mama were getting dressed. After tea [I] read. 14 degrees in the evening. N.P., Mama, Anya,

T., U., Olga, Pavl. Al.,[149] Kozhevnikov, Knyazich, Nastenka were making [pillows?] out of beans on the deck. Lots of fun. Poor Mama was tired. I think [her] heart was enlarged.

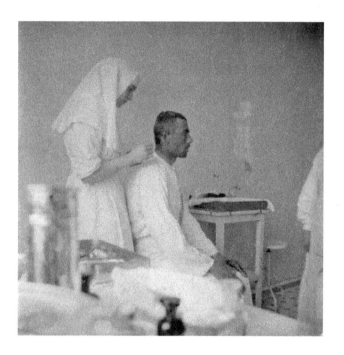

From the 1916 diary of Tatiana Romanov:

Monday, **13 June.** To Znamenie with Mama and to the infirmary. Colonel Zhuravsky of the 13th Belozersky Regiment—surgery. He was seriously wounded in the abdomen, chest and leg. Wrote, etc. Ate on the balcony. Wonderful weather. In the afternoon [we] lay out in the sun and picked flowers. At 6 o'clock rode with Isa. Papa

---

[149] Pavel Alekseievich Voronov, the officer who was Olga's love interest in 1913.

wrote. In the evening [went] to the infirmary without Mama. Sewed cushions until 11 o'clock. It is exactly a week that the little one left. May God save him. 9 [degrees] of heat.

From the 1918 diary of Nicholas II:

14 June. Thursday. Our dear Maria turned 19. The weather was still tropical, 26 degrees in the shade, and 24 degrees inside the rooms, so difficult to tolerate. Spent a disturbing night and stayed up, dressed... This all happened because the other day we received two letters, one after the other, where they notified us to be ready to be kidnapped by some loyal people! But they days passed and nothing happened, while the waiting and the uncertainty were very grueling.

From the 1913 diary of Maria Romanov:

15 June Saturday. In the morning stayed on the yacht. At breakfast sat with Nilov and Saltanov. In the afternoon went ashore played tennis and swung on giant steps. Had tea 4 with [illeg]. Read with Trina. At dinner sat with Babitzyn and Rodionov. In the evening talked with Pi and Nastenka.

1916 letter from Anastasia to Nicholas II:

16 June. My dear Papa Darling! I am writing out of turn as I did not have a chance to write because we were going to our new infirmary a lot. We already moved and it is terribly cozy. On the very first day they brought 3 officers there and 10 lower ranks, four of them seriously [wounded]. One boy, 16 years old, is also rather seriously wounded. On 14 June we had a real housewarming. We went to our infirmary 3 times, alone in the morning. In the afternoon with Mama and the sisters, and in the evening again alone, to a concert. It was very cozy, masses of people and wounded [were there]. But the funniest thing was when a 5-year-old boy Vitya (the son of our former wounded, who is now our banya attendant), he started to dance and everyone poked him and he got going, it was terribly funny, everyone was enjoying it and it was noisy and so forth, while he kept dancing calmly with his back to the public. When we were leaving, it was really cozy, as on the pink gangway they lit a lamp and there was pink light. [It was] awfully appetizing. Yesterday Count Grabbe came to [see] Vik. Erastovich and the Cossack who recently arrived wounded in his arm and hip, his name is something like Boyarkin. He is very merry and talks a lot. Now we feel sad passing by the old infirmary, the poor thing is just standing there, although there are 6 lower ranks [there] who do not get dressings and they are waiting to depart for Finland, so Maria and I go there, there are masses of workers and a lot of scattered things. Right now, the weather is sunny and warm, [but I] don't know what it will be like in the afternoon. Well, I must end. I send [you] a terribly big kiss, Darling Papa and Alexei 100000000 times. May God keep you, your loving loyal and faithful Kaspiyitz.

Letter from Maria to Nicholas II:

17 June, 1916. My dear Papa! Right now, I am sitting on the balcony with Mama and Anya. We just finished breakfast. The rain storm is everywhere, and the thunder is very loud. I don't know what we will do. These days Anastasia and I go to our new infirmary very often. It is awfully cozy. I hope that when you return you will come visit us [there]. Every evening we go to the sisters' infirmary, and there we play dobchinsky-bobchinsky.[150] You cannot imagine how Baron Taube bustles about and argues with Rita Khitrovo. They constantly exasperate each other. The lightning keeps flashing, and Anya crosses herself and

---

[150] A game.

says "Oy, please no, I don't want the storm." I will end my letter, as there is nothing more [to say]. I kiss you affectionately and Alexei. Please thank Zhylik for the letter. May God keep you. + Your Kazanetz.

From the 1913 diary of Olga Romanov:

Tuesday, **18 June.** Did not do anything in the morning. There were boating exercises. Papa kayaked. Warm wind, small waves. By breakfast time a tent was set up on the quarter deck. It was so cozy. In the afternoon [we] went ashore. Played 2 sets with Kozhevnikov against Zelenetzky and Neverovsky. After that he and Sablin taught me to walk on stilts, but nothing came of it. Returned earlier than usual and had tea in the saloon on the "Polar Star."[151] Then played with the officers on afterdeck. [It was] awfully hot. Mama did not come out for dinner. Her heart is still enlarged, No. 2 and a bit [more], and aching, which is why she spent the evening in bed. At 8 o'clock, a gale and heavy rain came out of nowhere, but then it cleared up. The balalaika players performed in the dining room. There was a gale again at a little past 10 o'cl. but then the wind subsided completely It is 19 degrees in my cabin, it's 11 o'cl. 12 min. now. Stood on the deck with Pavl. Al., Rodionov, Aunt Olga and T, chatted, laughed. Then Aunt went downstairs to Mama's, and we went in the control room because of the rain. Played with Pavl. Al. Akulina, fools and read fortunes for a bit. My dear N.P. is sad. May the Lord keep him. Moleben was on deck, but we did not go because of the rain—such a shame. The [mail] couriers leave on Tuesdays and Fridays.

---

[151] Yacht belonging to Dowager Empress Maria Feodorovna.

1915 letter from Tatiana to Nicholas II:

19 June. My dear darling Papa. Today we [sat] on the balcony after lunch, and as of today they wired us for electricity, and there are two lamps, which made it very cozy. This afternoon we were at the warehouse and worked. At 6 o'clock went to Anya's, the Cossacks were there, and then, incidentally, Colonel Kusov of the 1st Dragoon Moscow Regiment came over, your former Nizhegerodetz. He is very charming, as are all the others. Immediately he began to play with us, and we felt as if we had known each other for a long time— so sweet. When are You coming back Papa darling? I think it's time to come back to us! Huh? On Wednesday we had tea and Grandmama's on

Yelagin[152] and returned in a motor. Drove 1 hour 5 minutes. But we were not in a hurry, and then many streets in the city are being repaired, so you can only drive on one side [of the road]. Awfully stuffy in town, and I do not envy those who live there. Anya kisses Your hands. Went riding again. It was lovely. I pulled out my bed from behind the screen and slept in the middle of the room to get more air. Well, good-bye, Papa Darling, I kiss you very very affectionately. Your very loving and loyal to you Voznesenetz.

From the 1913 diary of Maria Romanov:

20 June Thursday. In the morning stayed on the yacht. At breakfast sat with Nilov and in the

---

[152] Yelagin Palace, home of the Dowager Empress Maria Feoorovna.

212

afternoon, went ashore, played tennis I with Zelenetzky, Anastasia and Arsenoev. Had tea 4 with Papa, Aunt Olga, ladies and officers who were on the shore. Read with Anastasia and Trina. Had dinner with Mama.

From the 1918 diary of Nicholas II:

21 June. Thursday. There was a change of commandants today – during dinner Beloborodov[153] and others came in and announced that instead of Avdeyev, the one who we mistook for a doctor has been

---

[153] Alexander Beloborodov, chairman of the Ural Regional Soviet.

appointed – Yurovsky.[154] During the day before tea, he and his assistants catalogued the gold jewelry – ours and the children's; the majority (rings, bracelets, etc.) they took with them. They explained that it was because there was an unpleasant incident in our house, mentioned our missing things. So, the suspicion about which I wrote on 28 May had been confirmed. I feel sorry for Avdeyev, it is not his fault that he was not able to hold back his people from stealing from the chests in the barn.

From the 1917 diary of Nicholas II:

---

[154] Yakov Yurovsky, the last commandant of the Ipatiev House and the chief executioner of the Romanov family.

22 June, Friday. Exactly three months since I came from Mogilev and here we are confined like prisoners. It is hard to be without news of dear Mama, but as for other matters, I am indifferent. Today the weather is still better—20 degrees in the shade, and 36 in the sun. There was a smell of fire in the air. After my walk, I took Alexei into my study, where it is cooler went over his history lesson and accomplished something. Alix did not go outside. Until dinner, the five of us were together. The weather was comparatively cool. The day passed as usual. Just before dinner came the good news of the launching of an offensive on the southwest front. IN the direction of Zolochev our troops, after two days of artillery action, broke through the enemy's positions and captured about 170 officers and 10,000 men, 6 cannons and 24 machine guns. The Lord be praised. God grand that this may be an auspicious hour. I felt altogether different after this cheering news

Tatiana to Countess Zinaida Tolstaya:

Tsarskoe Selo, **23 June 1917.** Dearest Z.S., I am terribly ashamed that I still have not thanked you for your letter on the 29th of May and the lovely embroidered bags. I kept the bluish one with multicolored flowers, Olga—the light blue one with yellow roses, Anastasia—the pink, and Maria—the all yellow. They are very useful to us and they always remind us of you. Mama always takes her bag to the garden with a book or something else. The weather here is warm all the time, then comes heavy rain and it becomes much fresher. But we needed the rain as it was very dry. How are you all? And what does your husband read aloud to you while you work? In the evenings after we have our dinner, we all work too while Papa reads to us. We are now finishing Volume VI of the book "Le Comte de Monte Cristo" by Alexandre Dumae [sic]. Do you know it? It is extremely interesting. Earlier we read about various detectives; which were also interesting. Well, goodbye, dear Z.S. I will wait for your letters. I kiss you affectionately and also Dalechka. Greetings to your husband and Seryozha. Take a photo all together and sent it to me please. I will be very glad to have it. Tatiana+

Letter from Anastasia to Nicholas II:

24 June, **1916**. Tsarskoe Selo. My dear Papa darling.

Mama and I just rolled around in the grass in front of the balcony. It was terribly pleasant and now I am the color of raspberries. We are waiting for Mama and the sisters for breakfast. Sashka will have breakfast with us today. Next to me on the table are your and Alexei's letters, which were just brought to us. I think that Maria wrote you that we have a new officer at our infirmary from the 10th Sharpshooter regiment, he is wounded in the arm, his name is Zhilinsky, I think, he is sweet although we don't know him well yet. Vik. Erast. is fussing about when and how the 1st Hundred will arrive. Yesterday we four started a bonfire and jumped over it. It was wonderful. We cut off old branches with dull knives and with our hands, and then swung in hammocks. Now there are two hammocks, as Marie has one too and they are hanging in a kilivatorny [?] column. Do you remember that yesterday was 3 years since we had the evening picnic in the Skerries and we all danced and Artemov told [us] all kinds of stories. I read my diary and therefore was reminiscing about every little detail from beginning to end. It was so nice then!!! Everything is as always now. I had a cold and a cough, I was so embarrassed because it is not supposed to happen in the summer, but it's a bit better now. So, at this moment I just sneezed, you tell me "Bless you," I am very grateful to you for this. Well I will end my letter with masses of kisses to you and Alexei 1000 times. May God be with you. Sleep well. Your loving. Your loyal and faithful little Kaspiyitz.

1915 letter from Olga to Nicholas II:

25 June. My Golden Papa! Didn't get the chance to write you with today's feld-yeger,[155] since there was no time. We went to the Grand Palace infirmary today with Alexei, and it was amazingly boring and lame, as we and the sisters stood by one tree, and the patients by another, and could not part for a long time. After

---

[155] Literally means "field huntsman."

that we played a game of tennis for the first time since Your departure. Four nets all different and I lost them all. The weather was wonderful, and the sun was very strong, so we are slowly getting tan, and the evenings are so cool, so that it's cold to sit outside in a dress. Here on the balcony it got very cozy ever since Mama acquired the new wicker furniture made by the invalids, and the two lamps stay lit. Now the tea table was brought in, and Galkin is fixedly shoving Anya's wheelchair under the table. Papa darling, I think about you so much during these anxious days. God willing, everything will become "more lighthearted," as Grigori always says. Oh yeah! We 4, Isa, Kira and Vilchkovsky went to Kolpin yesterday. It is much warmer there than here, and really beautiful near the river. We went to six infirmaries and a church where the image of Nikolai Chudotvorets[156] is. There were rather a lot of workers and among engineer-mechanics [was] Solovyov—remember him from the yacht, and then on "Abrek." I apologize for the ink smudge I just made. Kolenkin is at our infirmary—his left ear is infected, but he is better. He arrived to the Alexandrisky regiment for only a week, but everyone loved him very much and he is revving to return. Well,

---

[156] St Nicholas the Miracle Worker

I am ending now. May He keep you, Papa, my angel. I kiss you and love you very very much. Your loyal Elisavetgradetz. Regards to Nikolai Pavlovich.

From the 1917 diary of Nicholas II:

26 June/9 July, Monday. It was a glorious day. Our good commandant, Colonel Kobylinsky,[157] has asked me not to shake hands with the officers in the presence of outsiders, and not to greet the soldiers. There have already been several occasions when they refused to answer. Worked with Alexei in geography.

---

[157] Colonel Evgeny Kobylinsky, commander of the special detachment who oversaw the imprisonment of the imperial family.

We sawed up an enormous pine not far from the green-houses. The soldiers themselves, volunteered to help. The evening ended with reading.

From the 1913 diary of Olga Romanov:

Thursday, **27 June.** Went to the flag ceremony for the first time this year. At 8 o'cl. 15 min., Papa, Aunt Olga, and the officers took the "Razvedchik," which was docked at port, at the quarry. From there they walked 15 miles to the telegraph, went swimming and came back for breakfast. I sat on the deck, read. The deck tent was set up: starboard 23, portside 20. [They] held boating exercises. Pavl. Al. is on watch duty. Sat with N.P. at breakfast. In the afternoon everyone went ashore. I remained with Mama. She was lying down on the quarterdeck starboard, [was] very tired. Stayed there until 10 o'cl. [It was] windy and hot, 20 degrees inside the cabin. Poor Mama's heart is 2 and constant backache, does not stop for a minute. May the Lord save her. N.P. also sat there. Anya came out. After 6 o'cl. I read on deck. When Pavl. Al. came, we went to the top control room, where he was filling in the log journal, and I was dictating. Sat there together until 7 o'cl. Then he went to the saloon for dinner, not with us, since he had to write down the interrogation. Received cargo. Kokovtsov arrived on "Roksana" with a report for Papa. Aunt Olga left—[it was] so sad. Tomorrow at 6 in the morning they are leaving for Kronshtadt.[158] In the evening sat with Pavl. Al. (so nice) and Rodionov between telegraph room and chimney. Migalov was there too. Mama left early. Papa read in his cabin downstairs. Beautiful sunset.

---

[158] St. Petersburg's main seaport and naval base.

From the 1915 diary of Olga Romanov:

Sunday. **28th June.** During the day ate on the
balcony with A., M., and T. At 5 o'cl. went to meet
darling Papa. I am so happy that he is here. Until 10
o'cl. sat on the balcony—raining heavily.... Lord save
us.

From the 1916 diary of Maria Romanov:

29 June. Went to obednya 4 with Mama at the Palace infirmary. Had breakfast 4 with Mama, Isa is on the balcony. Before that rode with Shvybzik and Trina. Went to the new infirmary of the Svodny regiment No. 36 with A. Went to the new infirmary with A. Sat with Shurik too. Had tea with Shvybz and the same swung in a hammock. Rode with A. and Isa. Had dinner 4 with Mama on the balcony. Went to the sisters' infirmary. Played croquet and Dobchinsky-Bobchinsky.

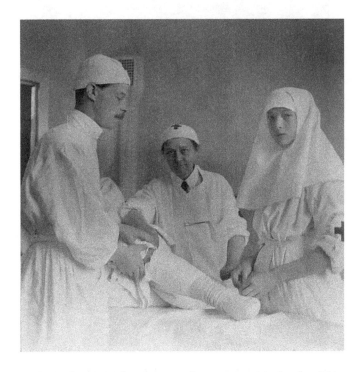

1916 letter from Tatiana to Nicholas II:

30 June. My dear Papa. Just said goodbye to the officers of the 4th Hundred, and tomorrow will go to moleben and see them off. It is so nice when every time we go out to the entrance and see all the wonderful Cossacks all bearing standards. Saw Alexander Konstantinovich from afar, he lost weight poor thing, after an illness. Uncle Georgi had breakfast with us. Tomorrow [he] is going to You. I am very happy that maybe we will see each other soon. Old Aunt Olga is going to Grandmama's in Kiev for about 10 days. Grandmama invited her. Then she said that Nicky and Andrei will come soon, so she is very happy. Did you walk a lot with Petrovsky? Who will be with You in his stead?... Today Baron Taube had surgery. His leg hurts terribly, poor thing. [There are] many new seriously [wounded], who were brought in by Princess Gedroitz[159] from the positions, but these brave lads endure [well]. Must end as Mama is waiting to send the letters. Christ be with You. I embrace [you] both. Your Voznesenetz.

---

[159] Princess and physician Vera Ignatievna Gedroitz.

JULY

From the 1916 diary of Maria Romanov:

1 July. Had lessons. Rode with Anastasia and Trina. Breakfast 4 with Mama and Isa on the balcony. In the afternoon went to our infirmary with A. Sat as usual. Went 4 to the farewell molebna. The 4th Hundred rode on vetka[160] and they passed by us, and we bid [our] farewells. Had tea 4 with Mama on the balcony. Rode with A. and Trina. Had dinner 4 with Mama and Zhylik on the balcony. Went to the sisters' infirmary. Played croquet and D.[obchinsky].-B.[obchinsky].

From the 1913 diary of Olga Romanov:

Tuesday. **2 July.** Stayed in bed half the morning. Went to play tennis in the afternoon. Bowled with Nastenka, Drenteln[161], Mochalov and Sablin. It was boring. Did not get a chance to sit with Pavl. Al. I was lying in the grass. Papa played with Poupse, Rodionov

---

[160] The train.
[161] Alexander Alexandrovich Drenteln, the tsar's Major-General.

and Melnitzky (from the "Turkmenetz"). After tea sat with Pavl. Al. in the control room and dictated the log journal to him. It was nice to sit on the sofa with him. Right before dinner strong wind and very heavy rain started, but it soon subsided. In the afternoon Mama was lying down on the quarterdeck. She did not come out in the evening. She feels a little better but not much. In the evening stayed on deck with N.P., then he, I, Nastenka, Pavl. Al., Rodionov and Kozhevnikov played different card games in our control room. It was lots of fun. Papa played kosti with Zelenetzky, Zlebov and Drenteln.

From the 1916 diary of Maria Romanov:

3 July. Went to obednya with Mama at the Pal. Infirmary. Rode with A. and Trina. Had breakfast 4 with Mama and Anya on the balcony. Went to our infirmary with Anya. Sat as usual. Had tea and dinner 4 with Mama on the balcony. Rode with A. and Shura. Went to the sisters' infirmary and played croquet and D.B.

From the 1915 diary of Tatiana Romanov:

Saturday, **4 July.** [Was] lying down in the morning.... Drove to the infirmary. Dressings... Sat with the Yerevantzy. Breakfast with Papa, Mama, Groten and Count Fredericks. Lesson in the afternoon. Then [I] was lying down on the balcony, then upstairs. Had tea with Papa and Mama. Went to vsenoshnaya. Dinner all together. Anya and Groten. Sat on the balcony.

From the 1917 diary of Nicholas II

5/18 July, Wednesday. It rained all morning; by 2 o'clock the weather improved; and toward evening it grew cooler. Spent the day as usual. In Petrograd there are disorders these days, accompanied by shooting. Many soldiers and sailors arrived there yesterday from Kronshtadt to oppose the Provisional Government. Absolute chaos. Where are those people who could take this movement in hand and put a stop to strife and bloodshed? The seed of all this evil is in Petrograd and not everywhere in Russia.

6/19 July Thursday. Fortunately, the overwhelming majority of troops at Petrograd remained loyal to their duty and order is again restored in the streets. The weather has been wonderful. Took a nice walk with Tatiana and Valia. During the day we worked successfully in the forest grove chopping down and sawing up four trees. In the evening I began...[sic]

From the 1916 diary of Maria Romanov

7 July. Arrived in Mogilev. Papa and Alexei came [to meet us]. Had breakfast all together. Rode in a motor across Dnieper to the other bank. Had tea in the train. Had dinner at Stavka on the balcony. Sat with Uncle Sergei and Father Shavelsky. Returned to the train and Papa too, and then he returned home and went to bed.

From the 1917 diary of Nicholas II:

8th July. Friday. Beautiful day; took a walk with pleasure. After breakfast found out from Count Benkendorf that we are not being sent to the Crimea but to one of the far away provinces, three or four days' worth trip east! But where exactly they won't tell us, and even the commandant doesn't know. And we really expected a long stay in Livadia! Cut down and felled a huge pine tree on the glade path. There was a short warm rain. In the evening I am reading "A Study in Scarlet" by Conan Doyle, aloud.

From the 1916 diary of Maria Romanov:

9 July. Wrote in the morning. Picked flowers in the field. Had breakfast at Stavka in a tent, sat with Uncle Sergei and Father Shavelsky. Rode in a motor ferry upstream on Dnieper. Got off to walk. Went to vsenoshnaya. Had dinner on the train. Walked near the train, shot from a revolver at Yulia (Isa's maid).

From the 1917 diary of Nicholas II:

10th July. Monday. ... [took a] morning walk around the entire park. During the day cut down four dry pine trees and cut them up right there for firewood. Returned home exactly at 5 o'cl. Read a lot. Before dinner Olga received gifts...

From the 1915 diary of Olga Romanov:

Saturday, **11ᵗʰ July.** [Olga's name day]. We 2 and Al. to the infirmary. From there to Znamenie. Changed dressings... At 12 ½ had moleben for me. Grandma had breakfast. Sat on the balcony with Mama and wrote telegrams. Very warm—14 deg. In the evening went to vsenoshnaya. Later, we 3 with Papa and Mama to Pavlovsk. Sat on the balcony with T., Aunt Olga Mavra, Ioannchik[162].... and Elena.[163] Came home at 11 o'cl. Save us, Holy Lord.

---

[162] Nickname for Prince Ioann Konstantinovich.
[163] Princess Elena Petrovna, wife of Prince Ioann Konstantinovich.

From the 1916 diary of Tatiana Romanov:

Tuesday, **12 July**. ... Mama and the sisters came and we went to eat breakfast with Papa on the balcony. It is raining. Later 4 went with Papa in the motor out of Mogilev to a very beautiful place. Got out and walked in the woods. Very nice. The rain stopped. Walked with Papa and Prince Eristov. Others were there. Returned at 5 o'clock. All had tea at Papa's in the dining room. Alexei got up, 36.8. At 5.40 we all drove to the train. Said goodbye to everyone and departed. Very sad to leave Papa and Alexei. It was so nice to be with them these few days...

From the 1917 diary of Nicholas II:

13th July. Thursday. In the last few days bad news has been coming from the south-west front. After our offense at Galich, a lot of regiments infected by the ignoble defeatist preaching, not only refused to move forward but in some areas retreated without even any pressure from the enemy. Taking advantage of this beneficial for them circumstance, the Germans and the Austrians broke through southern Galitzia despite low army strength, which may force the entire south-western front to retreat east. Complete disgrace and despair! Today the Provisional Government finally announced that capital punishment has been instated against those on the military arena who are convicted of treason. I hope that these measures are not too late. The day stayed warm and overcast. Worked on the same spot on the side of the glade. Cut down three and cut up two felled timber logs. Slowly starting to pack clothes and books.

From the 1913 diary of Olga Romanov:

13 July. Saturday. At 10 1/2 T and I rode on horseback. I rode Regent. We went to the lower park, the English park and the large training ground, [we] were learning to make an entrance with Korzhavin.

Warm, sunny, windy. Had breakfast with Papa and Count Fredericks, Mama was in her study. In the afternoon [we] played tennis with Papa and Nastenka. I thought about the past, about my darling, it's so sad without him and the others. Had tea and dinner with Papa and Mama. In the evening talked to N.P. and Ippolit on the telephone. Mama's heart is almost 3, [she] does not feel well. Went to vsenoshnaya.

Letter from Tatiana to Alexei:

Tsarskoe Selo. **14 July, 1916**. Alexei, my little sweet darling. We are so lonesome here without you and Papa. It was so nice in Mogilev visiting you! The weather is warm. We are sitting on the balcony. I was just at the Grand Palace with Maria and Shvybz. Tell Papa that Nurse Mobushina is still cross-eyed. A lot of wounded were there. Some old colonel, a Siberian, your Godfather, is sending his regards to you and wishes you good health etc. Of course, I don't remember his name. Tell V.N. that there are a lot of wounded. A total of 48. They brought in 11 men yesterday, and all are bedridden. All of them are from outside of Riga from the Siberian regiments. Some of Grandmama's [too]. Ours are all fine. [They] ask about you a lot, and want to see you very much. Thank P.V.P.[164] for his letters and tell him that he can write more. Well, goodbye. Darling Alexei, may God keep You. I kiss you and Papa very very affectionately. [I] squeeze You in my thoughts and love you very very much. Yours, Tatiana. I hug [you] tightly.

---

[164] Pyotr Vasilievich Petrov, Russian tutor for the imperial children.

From the 1917 diary of Nicholas II:

15th July, Saturday. A warmer day. In the morning took a walk around the entire park with O., T., M., A., while Alexei played around the kitchen garden. With us was only one officer from the 3rd sharp.[shooter] regiment. Today [we] cut down seven trees near the little path. Worked well as a team. At 6 ½ went to vsenoshnaya. In the evening pasted photographs into my album. Started [reading] "The luck of the Vails" aloud.

16th July. Sunday. The morning was grey, but weather warm. At the end of obednya, father Belyaev as usual said very true words about the current times. During the day worked in the same spot. Processed yesterday's four and cut down four more spruces into one pile.

Before dinner took a walk with T. and M. the evening was magnificent.

17th July. Monday. The weather became wonderfully hot. Took a nice walk with Tatiana. The guards from the 1st sharp. regiment were in good order, also the guards from the 2nd sharp. Reg., which replaced them today. Sawed up yesterday's four spruce trees on the little path itself. It was hot to work. Took a bath in a tub before tea. Looked through old albums upstairs in my new study.

18th July. Tuesday. The weather remained wonderful, with a deep blue sky. The scent of linden blossoms caressed one's olfactory senses. Took a nice walk in the morning. During the day worked to the right of the little path near yesterday's spot. Fell four dead spruces, but processed only two for firewood as they were very large, and the sun baked [us] severely. Took a bath before tea.

19th July. Wednesday. Three years ago, Germany declared war on us; it seems like a whole lifetime ago, these three years! Lord, help and save Russia! + It was very hot. Took a walk with T., M. and A. Once again, the entire convoy of guards from the 3rd regiment. Worked on the same spot. Felled four trees and finished the pine trees which were felled yesterday. Now I am reading Merezhkovsky's novel "Alexander I."

1916 Letter from Maria to Nicholas II:

20 July. My precious Papa, almost forgot to write to you today, I must have confusion. We will go to the Grand Palace with Shvybzik now. The sisters are going to Petersburg, and after the Gr. Pal. we will go riding with Mama and Anya. An ensign from my regiment, Shtyrev, is a patient at our infirmary, he was wounded in the leg by an explosive bullet, but he can walk on crutches. He told [us] a lot about the regiment. Today it is awfully cold and damp, but we still have breakfast on the balcony, albeit in our coats. The motor was supposed to be here already, and it just arrived so I will run. I kiss you affectionately and warmly and squeeze you. May God keep you. Your Kazanetz.

From the 1913 diary of Olga Romanov:

Sunday. **21 July.** At 9:20 Aunt Irene[165] arrived. Papa, T and I went to meet her and took her to the farm. Went to obednya. Had breakfast and dinner with both Aunts and Papa. Had tea with them and Mama. Alexei got dressed. At 11 the yacht left Portsmouth. In the afternoon took a boat ride with M and A and 2 sailors. Papa and T went kayaking. Then [we] walked with Papa and did giant steps. In the

---

[165] Princess Irene of Prussia, sister of the empress.

evening worked upstairs at Mama's. Temperature 37.4. She is tired, but [looks] beautiful. 14 degrees in the evening.

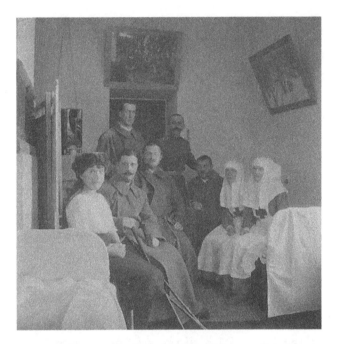

From the 1916 diary of Tatiana Romanov:

22 July. Went to obednya 4 with Mama. Breakfast on the balcony with the same. 4 with Mama went to the n[ew] infirmary for a concert. Had tea 4 with Mama and Uncle Nicky. Wrote telegrams, had dinner 4 with Mama and Anya. And went with A[nastasia] to the n[ew] infirmary, there was a play "An Evening at the Mansion of the Noblewoman XVII." Went to the sisters' infirmary, played ruble.

From the 1913 diary of Olga Romanov:

Tuesday. **23 July.** At 9 o'cl. 45 min T, Aunt Irene and I went to Tsarskoe Selo in a motor. Chief lady-in waiting Lori Yertsen went too. [We] inspected the regimental church and the Grand Palace. After that [we] went to [see] Aunt Miechen. Sat in her garden. Later Uncle Kirill and Aunt Ducky came over. Returned for breakfast. Uncle Andrei came over. In the afternoon we 5 dyed scarves downstairs on the balcony with Mama and the Aunt. Had tea and dinner with them. Papa went to Krasnoe Selo for camp inspection, a wrap-up, dinner and a theater performance. We all sat on the balcony and worked. There were so many flies, awful. No news from the yacht. 13 degrees. The sky is overcast, it drizzled.

From the 1914 diary of Nicholas II:

24th July. Thursday. Today Austria finally declared war on us. At this point the situation became completely clear. From 11 ½ had a meeting with the Advisory of Ministers on the Farm. Alix went to the city in the morning and returned with Victoria[166] and Ella. Besides them [we had over] for breakfast: Kostya and Mavra[167] who just returned from Germany and [who] also like Alek had difficulty passing the border. Warm rain all day. Took a walk. Victoria and Ella had dinner

---

[166] Victoria Battenberg, Alexandra's sister.
[167] Grand Duke Konstantin Konstantinovich ("KR") and his wife.

and then left for the city.

1916 letter from Maria to Nicholas II:

25 July. My dear Papa, I am so terribly happy to visit you and Alexei, after all you are so missed here. I have not packed yet, although not taking a lot of things with me, only the most necessary. I got a letter from N.D., will bring it with me and show it to you. [It] may be interesting for you. Yesterday we finally had a nice day, although not very hot but very pleasant, so a lot of wounded were lying outside. They brought three officers to us, 2 Keksumentzy and a Petrogradetz or a Muscovite. We saw them only for a few minutes as they just brought them in, and the doctor and Lazarev were with them. We had a very successful concert here at our infirmary on 22 July. Please thank P.V.P. for the letters. I will not have the chance to write to him. I kiss you and darling Alexei affectionately.

168

From the 1913 diary of Olga Romanov:

Wednesday. **26 July.** At 8 o'cl. saw AKSHV through the window. It was raining, but we two still went to Aunt's and walked with her in wet mud. Had breakfast with her and Papa. At 2 ½ Papa went to the camp for shooting [practice], etc. We 4 played a lot of tennis. Had tea and dinner with Mama and Aunt. Darling Mama has a severe headache. We all played cards with Aunt and laughed a lot. At about 7 o'cl. We and Aunt went to visit B.M. Talian in Strelna, viewed the gardens. Sunny and chilly. The yacht arrived in Oman for loading. Everything is well, thank

---

[168] An actual photograph from 26 July, 1913.

God. It is departing for Algiers in the evening.

"Saturday. **27 July**. Fireworks. We 2 walked around Peterhof with Aunt and Lori Yertsen. They took pictures of the most beautiful sites. Sunny. At 9 ½ Papa left for maneuvers and returned at 2 o'cl. Had tea with Papa, Mama and the Aunt. Had dinner with Mama and the Aunt. Papa had dinner with the French. [We] played tennis with Anya. It started to rain but then it ended. Went to church. Mama's face aches, but her head[ache] is better. Played cards and smoked."

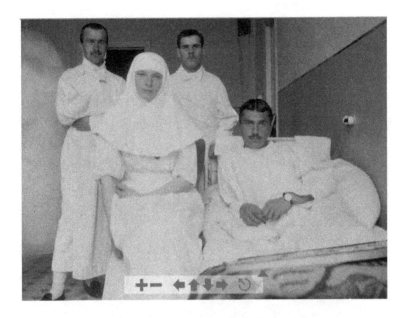

From the 1915 diary of Tatiana Romanov:

Tuesday, **28 July.** Lesson in the morning. Drove to the infirmary. Dressings... In between sat with Shakh-Bagov and others. Breakfast with Papa, Mama and Betsy Shuvalova. Lesson in the afternoon. Then we walked with Papa, and Mama in her carriage for the first time, to the Grand Palace. Had tea and lunch with Papa and Mama. After tea went to Anya's. The sisters rehearsed with Viktor Erastovich and Alexander Konstantinovich, and I encouraged them. Had a lesson. After lunch, spoke with Shakh-Bagov on the telephone. Papa read Chekhov.

From the 1917 diary of Nicholas II:

29th July. Saturday. The same beautiful weather. During the morning walk, while passing by the gates on the way to the orangery, we noticed a guard sleeping in the grass. Unter-officer who was escorting us came over and took away his rifle. During the day we cut down 9 trees and sawed up one pine tree—all right by the road. It was humid and cloudy, and thunder was heard, but the sky cleared up towards the evening. After vsenoshnaya Alexei got gifts. Cleaned up and packed my things, so now the rooms look so empty.

30th July. Sunday. Today dear Alexei turned 13 years old. May the Lord grant him health, patience, strength of character and body in these difficult times! Went to obednya, and after breakfast to molebna, where we brought the Znamenie Madonna icon. It felt especially nice to pray to her holy image with all our people. The marksmen of the 3rd regiment brought it and carried it away across the garden...

31st July. Monday. The last day of our stay at Tsarskoe Selo. The weather was beautiful. Worked in the same spot during the day; cut down three trees and sawed up yesterday's. After dinner waited for the appointed hour of departure, which kept being delayed. Unexpectedly Kerensky[169] arrived and announced that Misha will be coming soon. And in fact, around 10 ½ dear Misha came in, escorted by Ker.[ensky] and the chief of the guards. It was so nice to see each other, but it was awkward to talk in front

---

[169] Alexander Kerensky, head of the provisional government.

of outsiders. When he left, the sentry marksmen started to drag our luggage to the round hall. The Benkendorfs, ladies-in-waiting, chambermaids and our people were there too. We paced back and forth, waiting for the trucks to arrive. The secret about our departure was kept to a point where the motors and the train were ordered after our appointed departure time... Alexei wanted to sleep; he lay down then got up. A few times there was a false alarm, we put on our coats, came out on the balcony and returned to the halls. It got light [outside]. We had tea and finally at 5 o'cl. Kerensky appeared and said that we can go now. We climbed into two motors and went to the Alexander station. Climbed into the train at the crossing. Some kind of a Calvary team rode astride near us, all the way from the park. We were met by: I. Tatischev and two commissars from the government in order to escort us to Tobolsk. The sunrise was beautiful, at which point we started the trip towards Petrograd and via connecting path came out onto the Northern line. Departed T.[sarskoe] S.[elo] at 6.10 in the morning.

AUGUST

From the 1913 diary of Olga Romanov:

Thursday. **1 August.** At about 1 o'cl. [I] sat in Mama's bedroom and held a heating pad on Alexei's right arm. It hurts again. Had lessons. Had breakfast with Papa, the Aunt, Lori Yertsen and the Khan. In the afternoon visited an engraving factory with Papa and the Aunt. Rain, damp, chilly. Had tea and dinner with Papa, Mama and the Aunt. In the evening played cards. A telegram came at 5 o'cl. in the morning: the yacht had entered the Dardanelles. May the Lord save us. During dinner, Mama's face ached a lot. Poor Count Nirod is still not feeling well. Temperature 38 in the evening.

From the 1917 diary of Nicholas II:

2ⁿᵈ August. Took a walk before Vyatka, same weather and dust. By commandant's request had to close window shades at all stations; tiresome and foolish!

3ʳᵈ August. Passed Perm at 4 o'cl. and walked in the Kungur suburbs along the Sylva river, in a very beautiful valley.

170

4th August. Having passed the Urals, felt a significant coolness. Passed Ekaterinburg very early in the morning. All these days the second train with marksmen would catch up to us—we greeted [each other] like old acquaintances. Rode incredibly slowly, in order to arrive in Tyumen late, at 11 ½ o'cl. There, the train arrived almost next to the wharf, so we only had to walk down to the ship. Ours is called 'Rus." They started to load our things, which continued through the night. Poor Alexei went to bed God knows when again! Banging and pounding lasted all night and did not let me sleep. Departed from Tyumen

---

170 Contemporary photograph of Ekaterinburg.

around 6 o'cl.

5th August, Cruising down the river Tur. Slept a lot. Alix, Alexei and I each have a cabin with no facilities, all the daughters are together in a five bed [cabin], the suite is close by in the hallway; farther towards the bow is a nice cafeteria and a small cabin with a piano. The II class is under us, and all the marksmen of the 1st regiment who were on the train with us are downstairs in the back. Walked around upstairs all day, enjoying the air. The weather was overcast, but quiet and warm. In front of us is a ship and behind is another ship with the marksmen of the 2nd and 4th regiment and with the rest of the luggage. Stopped twice to load firewood. At night it got cold. Our kitchen is right here on the ship. Everyone went to bed early.

Dmitri Pavlovich to Nicholas II:

6 August, 1909. Stenkammar. Dear Uncle, I allow myself to pester you with a letter in order to ask if I may come to you in Peterhof with my sister. Maria received the invitation to come on the 15th of August. We are thinking of leaving Sweden on the 8th directly to Moscow to the Aunt (to pray to God with her at the monastery). We will stay there for about 4 days, and then, if you allow it, I will come to you too.

I only got to see the king and queen once here. This was on the 7th of August, new style, on the occasion of her majesty's birthday. This day was spent in

Stockholm, and not in Tulgarten, as the king could not leave the capitol due to strikes and anticipated unrest. Almost everyone in the city went back to work already, although the factories are still on strike. All the Swedes got terribly frightened when the strike began, and [they] sounded the alarm, but in the end, were afraid to do anything decisive. [My] time in Stenkammar went rather quickly. It was "cozy and charming." At first the weather did not spoil us, there was a lot of rain, but now it is nice. And now, in order not to remind you of Aunt Ella, I will end my letter and apologize for the annoyance. I kiss Aunt Alix's little hands. My heartfelt regards. Your Dmitri.

From the 1917 diary of Nicholas II:

7th August. Monday. Slept very well; woke up to rain and cold. Decided to remain on the ship. Some storms passed, but the weather got better by one o'clock. The crowds were still standing at the docks, their feet in the water, and [they] only ran under shelter when it rained. In both houses they are hastily cleaning and getting the rooms into presentable shape. All of us, including the marksmen, wanted to go somewhere farther down the river. Had breakfast at one, dinner at 8 o'cl., the kitchen staff is already cooking in the house, and someone brings our food from there. Walked around our cabins with the children all evening.   The weather was cold due to N-W wind.

171

8th August. Tuesday. Slept very well and got up at 9 o'cl. The morning was bright, later got windy, and again got hit with several storms. After breakfast went up the river Irtysh, about 10 versts[172]. Docked on the right shore and went out to walk. Walked by some hedges and having crossed the creek, we went up a

---

[171] Contemporary photograph of Tobolsk.
[172] A verst is an obsolete unit of length, equal to 3,500 feet or just over 1 kilometer.

high bank from where a beautiful view opened up. The ship came to pick us up and we headed back to Tobolsk. Arrived at 6 o'cl., to a different wharf. Took a bath before dinner, for the first time since July 31st. Thanks to that [I] slept wonderfully.

173

9th August. Wednesday. The weather still wonderfully warm. The suite spent the morning in town as usual. Maria had fever, Alexei had some pains in his left arm. Before breakfast I remained upstairs the whole time, enjoying the sun. At 2 ½ our ship moved to the other side and they started loading coal, while we went for a walk. Joy was bitten by a snake. It was too hot to walk. Came back to the ship at 4 ½ and returned to the old spot. The residents were boating and passed

---

173 Tobolsk street where the Governor's mansion (left) is located.

by us. The marksmen from our convoy "Kormiletz" moved into their town residences.

From the 1914 diary of Tatiana Romanov:

10 August—Sunday. In the morning went to obednya. Had breakfast 5 with Papa and Mama, Nik. Pav., Mordvinov and Anya. At 2 o'cl. we two with Mama rode to her community [organization] of the Red Cross for the farewell prayer service for the nurses who are going to the front. Then [I] wrote, later sat at Mama's. Had tea all together. Then Olga and I rode bicycles. Talked on telephone with Ya.P. and N.N. [We] 2 had dinner with Papa and Mama and Mordvinov. After that worked at our border, all is well thanks be to God.

From the 1917 diary of Nicholas II:

11th August. Friday. Alexei slept very little, he moved to Alix's room for the night. His ear got better, the arm still hurts a bit. Maria is better. The day was calm. Walked around upstairs all morning. During the day went up the river Tobol. Docked on the left bank, walked down the road and returned along the river with all sorts of difficulties, of the amusing sort. At 6 o'cl. arrived in Tobolsk and with a loud crack approached the ship 'Tovarpar", breaking our side plating on it. During the day it was really hot.

12th August. Saturday. Again an excellent day without sun, but very warm. In the morning walked around the deck and read there too until breakfast. Maria and

Alexei got up and went outside for fresh air during the day. At 3 o'clock went down Irtysh and docked at the base of a high bank, which we have been wanting to get to. Immediately climbed up there with the marksmen and then sat for a long time on a plain low stool, a wonderful view. Returned to Tobolsk during tea time.

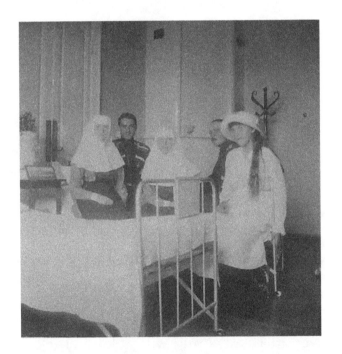

From the 1914 diary of Tatiana Romanov:

"Wednesday, **13 August**. In the morning two of us went to the hospital with Mama and Anya. [I] changed dressings on the same patient. Assisted others Went to [see] Cuirassier Karangozov. Mama was also changing dressings. Had breakfast 5 with Papa, Mama Aunt Elena and Uncle Nicky. During the day went to the tower with Papa. Went kayaking. Had tea and ate lunch with Papa and Mama. At 6 o'clock Princess Gedroitz lectured. After lunch spoke on the telephone with Nikolai Pavlovich."

From the 1913 diary of Olga Romanov

Wednesday. **14 August.** Livadia. Before 10 (when we went out to sea) Papa managed to go to the "Hollandia" to swim with a few officers. Brilliant transfer— banners were raised. The fleet and the batteries saluted. Had breakfast from 11 o'cl. 45 min. until 2, I think, when we arrived in Yalta. I sat in control room with S[174]. The Aunt, the sisters, Shura and Rodionov also came over there. It was sad and hard to part with my S. The honor guard was on the pier, etc. Had tea and dinner and spent the evening on the balcony. I kept looking at the yacht through the field glass—saw N.P. and S. 17 degrees in the evening. Went to vsenoshnaya, saw AKSHV. I am happy here but I would have been happier if I remained on the yacht. Mama's face aches again. Tiresome.

Thursday. **15 August**. Obednya was held at 11 o'cl. after which—breakfast with the suite. Zlebov, Stolitza, Nevyarovsky and Butakov were invited from the yacht.

---

[174] Pavel Alekseievich Voronov.

Saw S. for a moment through the field glass. I miss him so much at times, it's awful. In the afternoon walked to Oreanda on the horizontal path with Papa, the Aunt and M. Then we returned to the beach and went swimming. So pleasant. Had tea on the balcony. In the evening we 2 played poker with the Aunt. Mama worked. Talked to N.P. on the telephone. It rained a little, and we heard far away thunder. Sunny.

Letter from Anastasia to Nicholas II

16 August, 1916. My golden Papa darling! Thank you for the kisses in the letters. Today we got up rather late because no lessons. I already drove Mama and the sisters to the infirmary. The weather is really rotten and it is raining now and rather cold, only 10 degrees, and now this [kind of] weather is every day. Yesterday Aunt Miechen had tea with us, she returned recently and now lives in Tsarskoe. Yesterday morning we were riding and saw when the train from Mogilev arrived and saw Nilov and Voiekov—who came in a motor, it was very nice to see them. This afternoon we all and Mama, will go to the Grand Palace as we will take [photographs]—this is not so pleasant but that's the way it is. And in the morning Maria and I will go to our infirmary. [...]

From the memoirs of Anna Vyrubova:

"For the benefit of those who imagine that the work of

a royal nurse is more or less in the nature of play I will describe the average routine of one of those mornings in which I was privileged to assist the Empress Alexandra Feodorovna and the Grand Duchesses Olga and Tatiana, the two last named girls of nineteen and seventeen. Please remember that we were then only nurses in training. Arriving at the hospital shortly after nine in the morning we went directly to the receiving wards where the men were brought in after having first-aid treatment in the trenches and field hospitals. They had traveled far and were usually disgustingly dirty as well as bloodstained and suffering. Our hands scrubbed in antiseptic solutions we began the work of washing, cleaning, and bandaging maimed bodies, mangled faces, blinded eyes, all the indescribable mutilations of what is called civilized warfare. These we did under the orders and the direction of trained nurses who had the skill to do the things our lack of experience prevented us from doing. As we became accustomed to the work, and as both the Empress and Tatiana had extraordinary ability as nurses, we were given more important work. I speak of the Empress and Tatiana especially because Olga within two months was almost too exhausted and too unnerved to continue, and my abilities proved to be more in the executive and organizing than in the nursing end of hospital work. I have seen the Empress of Russia in the operating room of a hospital holding ether cones, handling sterilized instruments, assisting in the most difficult operations, taking from the hands of the busy surgeons amputated legs and arms, removing bloody and even vermin-infected dressings, enduring all the sights and smells and agonies of that most dreadful of all places, a military hospital in the midst of war. She did her work with the humility and the gentle tirelessness of one dedicated by God to a life of ministration. Tatiana was almost as skillful and quite as devoted as her mother, and complained only that on account of her youth she was spared some of the more trying cases. The Empress was spared nothing, nor did she wish to be. I think I never saw her happier than on the day, at the end of our two months' intensive training, she marched at the head of the procession of nurses to receive the red cross and the diploma of a certificated war nurse."

From the 1917 diary of Nicholas II:

17th August. Thursday. Magnificent day; 19° in the shade, 36° on the balcony. Alexei had pains in his arm. Spent an hour in the morning in the garden, and during the day- two hours. Yesterday started to read "L'ile enchantee'. In the evening played dominos: Alix, Tatiana, Botkin and I. During tea time there was a big rain storm. Moonlit night.

175

18ᵗʰ August. Friday. The morning was gray and cold, the sun came out around one, and the day became really nice. In the morning, Rita Khitrovo, who came from Petrograd, appeared in the street, and went to see Nastenka Hendr.[ikova]. This was sufficient for them to search her home in the evening. Devil knows what this is!

---

175 Countess Anastasia "Nastenka" Hendrikova, Romanov family friend. Followed them into exile and was also consequently killed by the Bolsheviks.

From the 1916 diary of Alexei Romanov:

"**19 August**. Had 2 lessons in the morning. Wrote to Mama before breakfast and took a walk. Had breakfast with everyone in the tent. In the afternoon rode down the Dnieper. In the evening listened to Sig's reading and studied with P.V.P. Went to bed early-ish."

From the 1917 diary of Nicholas II:

20ᵗʰ August. Sunday. Ideal weather: during the day the temp. reaches 21° in the shade. At 11 o'cl. obednitza[176] service in the hall. Found work for myself in the garden: cutting down a dry pine tree. After tea, as usual these days, read with the daughters on the balcony under the hot rays of sun. The evening was warm and moonlit.

---

[176] An abbreviated obednya service.

From the 1916 diary of Maria Romanov:

21 August. Went to obednya with Mama. Then said goodbyes at our infirmary with Shvybz. Boarded the train and went to Smolensk. Had breakfast, tea and dinner 4 with Mama, Isa, Resin, Lavrov, Zhylik and 2 engineers. Zhylik read "Anand ee monde s'enuie" to us.

From the 1913 diary of Olga Romanov:

Thursday. 22 August. Walked in the vineyard. Papa and I swam. The others have either a runny nose or Bekker. Clear warm water. Saw N.P. and S. through the field glass. Rodionov, Batushka,[177] Stolitza and S. had breakfast. Awfully happy to see him, [I] missed him so much. In the afternoon Papa went to Krasny Kamen. We four walked with Anya, Rodionov and S. It was very nice. Sat on the well under the balcony with my S. until 3 ½. The others sat on a bench. Then went to see Mama on the balcony. Alexei was

---

[177] A priest, literally translates to "Little Father."

there too. Accompanied them to Anya's [room], then they read. Had tea and dinner with Papa, Mama, the Aunt. In the evening Papa read. 18 degrees, summer lightning far away at sea. In the afternoon there was a thunderstorm in the mountains. [It was] sunny here.

From the 1916 diary of Maria Romanov:

23 August. Went to molebna. Then had breakfast at Hotel "Bristol" with the staff officers. I sat with Uncle Boris and Count Benkendorf. In the afternoon we went up the Dnieper. Ran around in the bushes. Had tea at Papa's. Went to a cinematograph, they showed the drama "Mystery of Nogorok" and others. Had dinner 4, while Mama [ate] with Papa and Igor. Mordvinov was here and we tormented him. Before dinner talked to Lavrov.

24 August. In the morning [we] wrote and sat in the field with the children. At breakfast in the tent, [I] sat with Uncle Georgi and Uncle Kirill. Went to the left bank in a ferry. 2 half-Hundred and 3 half-Hundred came there, officers Papasha, Ponkratov, Gramatin, Shkuropotsky, Kolesnikov and Ergushov. The Cossacks played various games, danced and sang, it was really nice. Then [we] crossed to the right side and ran around in the bushes there. On the way back [we] caught up with the Hundred which was walking along the bank and they rode along us while "djigiting."[178] Had tea at Papa's on the train. Had dinner 4, while Papa [ate] with Mama. Tormented and scared Toto, played hide and seek.

1915 Letter from Tatiana to Nicholas II:

25 August. My dear darling Papa. Writing to You in the morning before lesson. The weather is disgusting. Wind and rain, it will probably be like this until the

---

[178] Georgian tradition of doing acrobatics while galloping on horse

evening. How did You settle in, that is, not You, but where did the train stop, in the woods or where? Tomorrow I had a meeting of my Petrograd Committee. So tiring. Just now returned from the Grand Palace. One of the officers from my regiment is a [patient] there, and at our Palace infirmary there are two others also from my regiment. Last night we went with Olga before bed to see whether Alexei was sleeping. It turned out not. Then, to entertain him, we began to sing the songs "Manglisi to Tiflis" and still others, which the Yerevantzy taught us. But then he fell asleep, and we left. The weather is most disgusting—rain, wind, and generally revolting. Anastasia has recovered and already went back to the infirmaries. Today Elena had tea with us together with Vsevolod.[179] So touching, isn't? Please, regards to Nikolai Pavlovich. May God keep You. Very lonesome without you. I kiss and embrace you firmly and gently, darling Papa. Your Voznesenetz.

---

[179] Prince Vsevolod Ioannovich, son of Prince Ioann Konstantinovich and Princess Elena Petrovna

From the 1913 diary of Olga Romanov:

Monday. **26 August.** Stayed in bed for a long time. S., Zlebov, Batushka and Stolitza had breakfast. Then [we] went to the Aunt's with S. and Zlebov and stayed with her for a while. She took pictures of us. It was so nice. In the afternoon [I] stayed home, and was happy about it. Papa, Aunt and A went to Simeiz to [see] Maltzev. I read on the balcony. Then N.P. arrived. Sat with M who is in bed, Mama too. Had tea in the sitting room. At 6 ½ we two went to Yalta with Anya. Walked along the waterfront, stopped by an apothecary and a shop, where we bought a scarf for

Mama. Then went to the yacht in a horse-drawn cab. The crew walked along the pier, [I] saw everyone, but did not see anybody in town. It was lots of fun. On the way back ran into AKSHV in the vineyard. Had dinner inside since it's too chilly—13 degrees and windy. In the evening played cards. Papa read. Mama's heart No. 2.

1915 letter from Anastasia to Nicholas II:

27 August. I am still in bed while Mama and the sisters are going to church, I also would like to go, I already wrote to Mama to ask, but I don't know what the answer will be. Luckily today there is no wind and the sun is peeking out a little. Maria and I continue to sleep in the middle of the room and I don't think we will move from here as it is much better. In the morning we went to obednya and then to Mama's infirmary. In the afternoon we rode with Mama and Anya and ran into horrible old ladies [...] Now we are sitting around and Uncle Pavel will be here for tea. Maria was delighted because as we were leaving the church, the fat Demenkov was standing there, but no other good people were there. Alexei is playing now with the little Alexei and Sergei. I am sorry but I have to go to tea. All the very best. Regards to Nikolai Pavlovich from me. Sleep well. Do not tire yourself out too much. I wish you all the best. May the Lord be with you. I kiss you 10000000000 times. Your loving loyal and faithful daughter. Kaspiyitz. Nastaska. ANRIKZS.

From the 1913 diary of Olga Romanov:

Wednesday. **28 August.** Walked. Everybody went swimming, but I did not—waves and cold. N.P., Zlebov, Kublitzky and Shepotiev had breakfast. Went to [see] Madame Zizi, who is in bed. Played tennis in the afternoon. Played 1 set with Anya against Papa and T and lost. Then played one set with T against Anya and A and finally 3 sets with my S. against T and Rodionov, but won only 1. Mama sat there with N.P. Had tea in front of the house. Damp and cold. M is still in bed. Had dinner in the yacht saloon. [I] sat with Papa and N.P. Left the table at 10 o'cl. Stefanesko played a dulcimer. Remarkably cozy.

Stood on the deck with S. Suddenly everyone started dancing on starboard quarter-deck. It was such fun. Then [we] went on the cape, rode all around it in a wagon. When we returned, we resumed dancing—I danced a lot with the dearest S. At 12 o'cl. went downstairs and sat cozily by the engine hatch and listened to Stefanesko until 1 o'cl. in the morning. The Black Sea Fleet String Orchestra was playing on the deck. When we returned, Mama was in bed. May the Lord keep her.

1915 letter from Tatiana to Nicholas II:

29 August. My dear darling Papa. Mama just got your letter, we sat on the balcony and had tea. Wonderful weather. It was so nice last night, this general confession. I loved it and Batushka spoke remarkably well. Many people received communion. Then we, with Mama had tea on the balcony, then went to the infirmary, Alexei was in his protective and was very satisfied. Breakfast with Madame Zizi and Isa. Later rode in Pavlovsk. Mama with Anya in the front of the carriage, and we 4 in the rear. We drove on the same roads where we went with You in the evenings in the motor, and ahead of us was some civilian riding the middle of the road, the driver shouted to him to let us pass, he would not pull over so our horses took fright and rushed to the side in a ditch, as the road is very narrow. We jumped out, and half the carriage ended up in a ditch. The driver then shouted at him to get down and help us pull out the carriage and horses, which already started to thrust a little bit, but this idiot stopped his horse and in the most indifferent manner looked at us. When Mama heard that the driver was calling for help, she stopped and Konkov got down and ran for help. Mama was left alone in a carriage with Anya to hold back the horses. Konkov cursed this idiot as he passed him, but he just said, "Why curse" – and steadily kept going. He did not even bother to hold back the horses for Mama. Fool!

Our carriage had to ride in the field for a long time, as the horses were too scared to jump over the ditch, but later we successfully continued our walk. I am awfully glad to have my three Voznesentzy in our infirmary. But the fourth accidentally ended up at the Grand Palace. Tomorrow is my regimental holiday. Very lonesome without you, Papa darling. We had a moleben at our infirmary church, for the occasion of You taking over command. They are all terribly happy. Please give regards to Nikolai Pavlovich and Dmitri. Well, good-bye, good darling Papa. May the Lord help and keep You. I kiss You firmly and gently, as I love [you]. Your faithful Voznesenez. Forgive my terrible handwriting.

From the 1916 diary of Maria Romanov:

30 August. Went to obednya. At breakfast sat with Uncle Georgi and Dmitri. Went to the same place in motorboats. Children from the city garden were playing there. Returned during a rain storm. Had tea at Papa's. Went to [see] a cinematograph, the continuation of "Mystery of Nogork" and others. Had dinner 4 with Papa and Mama, Dmitri, Anya and Kiki[180].

---

[180] Nickname of Nikolai Pavlovich Sablin.

From the 1913 diary of Olga Romanov:

Saturday. **31 August**. Swam with Aunt for the last time. Only 13 degrees, took one dip in the water. Left at 10 ½. We two [rode] in 2 motors with Drenteln and Mordvinov. AKSHV came to bid farewell to Aunt, [I] greeted them. The turns were ghastly. Arrived at Bakhchisarai at 2 ½, had breakfast there in the house, walked in the garden and the cemetery. Went to the monastery on a cliff, very beautiful. Then walked uphill to old city of Gufut-Kale. Only two old men live there. Had tea in the garden under a chestnut tree. Left a little after 6 o'cl. Aunt Olga, the Princess[181] and Mordvinov stayed and waited for the train. It is so sad that she is leaving. Returned at 9 o'cl. with Drenteln and Stolitza. Foggy and cold on Ai-Petri. The moon. Mama's heart bothers her, she is tired. Saw my S. through the field glass, N.P. too.

---

[181] Dr. Vera Gedroitz.

SEPTEMBER

From the 1917 diary of Nicholas II:

1ˢᵗ September. Pankratov[182], the new Provis. Gov.

---

[182] Head of the guards in Tobolsk.

commissar arrived and settled in the suite house[183] with his assistant, some unkempt looking ensign. He has the look of a laborer or an impoverished teacher. He will act as the censor of our mail. The day was cold and rainy.

1915 letter from Tatiana to Nicholas II:

2 September. My dear darling Papa. I was awfully glad to get your telegram yesterday. Today we are going with Mama to Petrograd to the infirmary. It

---

[183] Members of the imperial suite who followed the imperial family to Tobolsk lived in Kornilov house located near the Governor's mansion. It can be seen on the right in the photo above, while the mansion is on the left.

seems that this is where they bring our prisoners. And then to Grandmama's for tea. Sitting now before the lesson until 9 o'clock. Wonderful weather, 22 degrees in the sun. Papa, where is it better to walk, in Mogilev or Baranovichi? Just returned from Petrograd, went to Grand Duchess Elena Pavlovna's clinic and saw a lot of wounded, who were just brought in today. They were all happy to finally arrive here. Went to Grandmama's. Aunt Ksenia's boys returned from the Crimea. Feodor[184] it seems has grown and got thinner, as he was ill. We have already started lessons on winter schedule, so I now have a lesson at 8 o'clock. Sorry, that this letter is so stupid and uninteresting. May God keep You. I kiss you very very affectionately, how I love [you]. Your Voznesenetz. Regards to Nikolai Pavlovich.

---

[184] Prince Feodor Alexandrovich.

From the 1913 diary of Olga Romanov:

Tuesday. **3 September.** Had religion and French lessons. Then [we] went to the beach with Papa and swam. 15 degrees in the water. Saw S. through the field glass. N.P., Ippolit, Batushka and Rodionov had breakfast. Played tennis in the afternoon. Played 2 sets with N.P. against S. and T. I started out badly without S., and that's why [we] kept losing. Lost 1 set with Anya against Papa and T, and lost again with N.P. against Rodionov and T. Mama was there too. Petrovsky [too]. Had tea in the garden. I sat with S. It was nice but sad. At 6 o'cl., read. Had dinner on the balcony. After that rode to Ai-Todor in a motor with Papa, T and Anya. [Someone] was shooting rockets across the road. Drove to the yacht and then turned around to go back. S. was on watch duty. Mama's temperature is 37.3. Chilly, quiet, nice. The moonlight.

From the 1916 diary of Maria Romanov:

4 September. Went to obednya. Wrote to Zhylik. Papa was at the Headquarters. At breakfast sat with Dmitri and Uncle Sergei. Rode to the upper bridge in motors and walked. Had tea in the train. Said goodbye to Papa, Alexei, and the children whom we pushed into a hole in the ground and left. Had dinner 4 with Isa, Kiki, Khodarsky, Ergushev, P.V.P. and the engineer. P.V.P. read to us.

1916 letter from Alexei to Empress Alexandra:

Mogilev. **5 September.** My dear Mama. It is so empty
without you and boring. Today the sky is blue and it's
15° in the sun. The cat is lying on the couch, and Joy
was searching for fleas on her and tickled her
frightfully. If you need for Joy to look for fleas on you,
I can send him, but that will cost you 1 r.[uble]. I will
have 2 or 3 lessons. Will pray for you and the sisters.
May God keep you!   Yours, A. Romanov

Letter from Maria to Alexei:

Tsarskoe Selo. **6 Sept., 1916**. My darling little soul, Alexei! You cannot even imagine how boring it is to be back at Tsarskoe. Today, when I just woke up, I was really surprised to be back in my room. I saw you in my dream, as if we never left you. The head of the infirmary, Baron Kaulbars, also wanted to be in the photo and sat on the little table which you [would normally] put near on a bed. Of course, the table couldn't hold him, one leg broke, and he fell, it was all very funny. I kiss you and dear Papa affectionately. Your sister Maria. May God keep you.

From the 1917 diary of Nicholas II:

7th September. Thursday. The morning was cloudy and windy, later the weather improved. Were outside a lot; filled up the duck pond and sawed some firewood for our baths.

8th September. Friday. For the first time went to Blagoveschenie church[185], where our priest has been serving for a while now. But my joy was spoiled by the foolish circumstances during our procession over there. Along the path of the town gardens stood the marksmen, and by the church was a huge crowd! This deeply disturbed me. The weather was nice, a little cool.

---

[185] Chapel near the Governor' mansion where the captive imperial family was allowed to worship.

Letter from Nicholas II to Tatiana:

Mogilev. **9 September, 1915**.   Dearest Tatiana, I thank you very much for your lovely letter. I am pleased to receive them together with the letters of dear Mama—from the daughter on duty. - Here, although U.[ncle] Boris, U. Georgiy and Dmitri are here with me now, I am still bored here without you and sometimes feel lonely. Time passes very quickly. I am busy all morning at the headquarters with my good general Alekseev until breakfast. After eating, I'm in a hurry to finish the paperwork, as the train leaves at 3 o'clock. I then leave in the motor, sometimes [go] far away and walk along the highway. Have tea with the gentlemen and study before lunch. In the evenings I either write to Mama or play dice in a small room next to the dining room. The view of the Dnieper from there and of the other bank is very beautiful. Generally speaking, all the areas of Mogilev are picturesque and you all would have liked them ... Your telegram about the scandal that happened with Ortipo had me very amused—I imagine what it would be like... the little monster! Today passing one village, at low speed, hit a very fat pig, which ended up under the motor [car], because it got scared of a big dog. She immediately got up and let out a squeal and galloped home; with a little blood dripping from her snout! The weather is now cold, but the barometer rises, hopefully it will be Indian summer. I have not heard anything about A.[unt] Olga! Well, goodbye. I embrace my dear Voznesenetz. Christ be with you. + Your Papa. Do not respond to me with a telegram.

From the 1913 diary of Olga Romanov:

Tuesday. **10 September.** Had lessons, after that went swimming with A and Papa. 18 ½ degrees. S., Kublitzky, Ippolit and Babitzev had breakfast. Tennis in the afternoon. Played 4 sets with Rodionov: 2 against Papa and Butakov, and won 1. 2—against Papa and Anya, and won both. It was fun, but [I felt] empty and sad without my beloved S. N.P. also was there, [he] sat with Mama. Had tea in the garden—warm. Had dinner on the balcony. Warm. Evening lightning far away. Papa read, we worked. Mama's heart aches and she does not feel well. Spoke on the telephone with Papa [sic?].

From the 1914 diary of Tatiana Romanov:

Thursday, **11 September.** Had a lesson in the morning. Went to Znamenie, from there to our infirmary. Dressings... Then went to see everyone again, and sat on the third ward. Had breakfast 5 with Papa and Mama. In the afternoon 3 with Papa rode bicycles. Mama, Olga [were] in Petrograd. The dentist came over. Had tea upstairs. Then Mama, Olga and I went to Realnoe School inside of which there was a moleben for the wounded. Had dinner with Papa and Mama. Spoke with Nikolai Pavlovich on the telephone.

From the 1917 diary of Nicholas II:

12ᵗʰ September. Tuesday. Warm gray day. During the day sawed firewood and the daughters played with tennis balls on the wooden sidewalk.

From the 1914 diary of Tatiana Romanov:

Saturday, **13 September.** Had a lesson in the morning. Saw Nikolai Pavlovich for one minute. Then to Znamenie, from there to our infirmary. Today we had two surgeries, my Girsenok from yesterday, they cut his leg and removed fractured pieces of bone, and then Olga's Ogurtsov [they did] the same from his right palm. Then [we] sat on the third ward. Went to see the rest [of the wounded]. Breakfast 5 with Papa, Mama and Count Fredericks. In the afternoon walked

4 with Papa, Mama [rode] next to us in a charabanc.[186] Had tea upstairs. Had a lesson. Went to vsenoshnaya. Had dinner 4 with Papa, Mama and Resin.

From the 1913 diary of Maria Romanov:

14 [September]. Saturday. In the morning went to obednya with Papa. At breakfast sat with Lavrinovsky and Komarov. In the afternoon played tennis 4 with Papa, Mama, Anya, Kiki, Babitzyn, Kolya and Ippolit were there. Had tea in the little house. Went 4 to vsenoshnaya. At dinner sat with Apraksin and Nilov. Listened to Stefanesko.

---

[186] A carriage.

From the 1913 diary of Olga Romanov:

Monday. **16 September**. Studied. It was cool out in the sea. At 11:38 we two went in motors to Kosmodemyansky with Papa and Drenteln. Saw S. on the seafront. I felt awfully happy. We [had to] stop on the way because T wasn't [feeling] well. After 12 o'cl. we passed by Alushta. Arrived at 2 o'cl. 15 min., ate, and then Papa went hunting. He returned at 7 o'cl. Picked dogwood berries with Drenteln and Shura. Made cookies and jam on the porch. It's warm in the sun, 16 degrees. It is so beautiful here. Alma is rumbling down there. Walked after tea. Before dinner and before evening we 2 played kosti[187] with Papa and Drenteln. Mama talked on the telephone. We 2 sleep in the same room with Shura. Cold. Walked until it got dark. Stars. Clear.

Letter from Anastasia to Nicholas II:

17 September, 1916. My good Papa Darling! This morning we had a light but nasty snow, and now it's sunny but cold. [...] We are [the same] as usual. The other day we played tennis with our wounded officers,

---

[187] A game. The word translates to "bones."

they play rather well now as they practice every day.

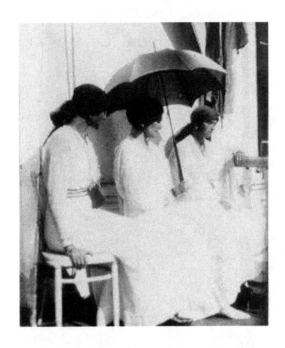

Tatiana to Grand Duchess Ksenia Alexandrovna:

18 September, 1917. Tobolsk. My dear sweet Godmother. Finally got a chance to write and thank you for the card. Last, I wrote to you was from the steamer named after Sof.[ia] Dm.[itrievna]. Did you get it? We telegraphed N.A. around the 15/VIII where we congratulated them with the birth of their son—I do not know whether it reached [them]. I would be terribly pleased if you wrote to me, address it to me directly or to Commissar Pankratov, through whom all correspondence passes; whichever you prefer. Well, then. The weather here is wonderful every day, and today it is about 18 deg. in the shade. So nice, we sit a lot in the garden or in the front yard, where they fenced in part of the street for us, behind which is the town garden. All the roads, that is the streets, are wooden planks and in many places the boards have rotted and [there are] big holes. Luckily no-one fell in. But during rain it is very slippery. – It is awfully pleasant to have a balcony here where we see the sun shining from morning 'til night. It is fun to sit there and watch the street, to see the people walk by. That is our only amusement. We now have a whole farm here. Lots of chickens, turkeys, ducks and five pigs, a cat, [they all] live in the former governor's stables. One accidentally escaped and ran to the street. Looked for him for a long time but could not find, and then in the evening he came back to us himself. Alexei feeds all the animals every day. He and Papa dug a small duck pond, where they swim with pleasure. From our windows [we have] a beautiful view of the mountains and the upper [part of] town, where there is a large Cathedral. [illeg] ... arranged to play gorodki in front of the house, and we play [a game] something like tennis, but of course without a net, but just for practice. Then we walk back and forth, in order not to forget how to walk. – The length of 120 steps, much shorter than our balcony. – On Sundays we have obednitza in the hall, [we] went to church twice. You can imagine what joy it was for us after 6 months, as you remember how uncomfortable our camp church was in Ts.[arskoe] S.[elo].

The church here is nice. One big summer [area] in the center, for the parish service, and two winter ones on the sides. In the right aisle they had service for us alone. It is not far from here, we have to walk through town and directly across the road. We rode Mama in a wheelchair, as it is difficult for her to walk. It is sad that she has severe pains in her face all the time, apparently from her teeth, and then from the dampness. But all the rest [of us] are healthy. I hope

that all of you are too. How is little Tikhon[188], his
parents? Did Aunt Olga get my letter from 6/IX? How
are your granddaughter and all the children? And You
yourself, how do you feel? What do you do all day—
how do spend your time? Did Grandmama recover?
Tatischev was very touched that he was remembered.
– We sit all together in the evenings, someone reads
aloud. We eat breakfast together too but have tea by
ourselves. We remember you all very often. Would so
much like to see you and talk. Have not seen each
other for so long and so much time has passed. –

189

Have you heard about the wedding of little Maria P.
and Gulya P. We really did not expect this—and you?

---

[188] Tikhon Nikolaevich Kulikovsky, son of Grand Duchess Olga Alexandrovna.
[189] Contemporary photo of Tobolsk.

Oh, sorry, I fibbed, the last time I wrote to you was 17 / VIII. How is Sonya's health. Have you heard where Sasha M. (daughter of Baby L.) is now and what is she doing these days. Do you drive around the neighborhood or to Yalta. I will wait for the letters from you. All the best. May Lord bless you all. We kiss you all very affectionately, the same as [we] love [you]. [We] pray for you. Your very loving goddaughter Tatiana

From the 1913 diary of Olga Romanov:

Thursday. **19 September.** Walked to church via the horizontal path with Papa and smoked on a bench in Livadia. Stolitza, Shepotiev, Kozhevnikov and

Batushka, as well as the Georgian regiment delegation, had breakfast. Tennis in the afternoon. Played 4 sets against Rodionov and T., 2 sets with N.P., we lost. Also played 2 sets with Papa. We lost one, and they lost one. Butakov was there too, as well as Mama. Alexei's right arm hurts. Did not see S., and I feel lonesome. Papa read Teffi, Mama and we worked.

190

Letter from Maria to V.G. Kapralova:

To: Vera Georgievna Kapralova, Sister of Mercy at [Feodorovsky] Infirmary in Tsarskoe Selo. Tobolsk.

20th September, 1917. I thank you very much, my sweet Vera Georgievna, for the card. I was

---

190 The grand duchesses' room at the Governor's mansion.

remembering you on the 28th of August in particular. It was so nice at the infirmary. We remember you all of you very very often. Do you ever see the former nurses and Olga Vasilievna? Please pass this letter to Katya. All this time we've had wonderful weather and [it is] even hot in the sun. But today it is snowing and strong wind. Right now, I am sitting in my room. We live in one room all 4, so it is not lonesome. Our windows look over the street and we often look at the passers-by. Well, and what do you do my dear?

I continue writing on **21st September**. The snow is already sitting on the road. And what kind of weather do you have? Is it still warm or cold already? I remember how we used to go to this infirmary last year. – Did you finish embroidering your appetizing blue pillow case with the grapes? Anastasia kisses and thank you for the card, she will write one of these days. We just took a walk, went to the garden and dug for rutabaga. Here in the garden we only have rutabaga and cabbage. Thank Verochka and Evg. Aleks. very much for the remembering [us], we kiss them affectionately. Do you know anything about the health of Anna Pavlovna? Forgive me for so many questions, but I want to know so much what everyone is doing and how they all are. I wish you all the best, my dear, and embrace you warmly. I hope that you got our letter in time for the holiday. Heartfelt greetings to your sister and all the acquaintances. Does Kolibri and others write to you? How did they settle in at the Infirmary No.36? Probably it is very cozy, were you there? Well time to end. M.

From the 1913 diary of Maria Romanov:

21 September. Saturday. In the morning had lessons. Went to the beach with Trina. Had breakfast with Papa and Mama on the sofa. In the afternoon played tennis 4 with Papa. Mama, Anya, Kiki, and Zlebov were there. Had tea at tennis. Went to vsenoshnaya. At dinner sat with Konsdadi[illeg] and Niko.

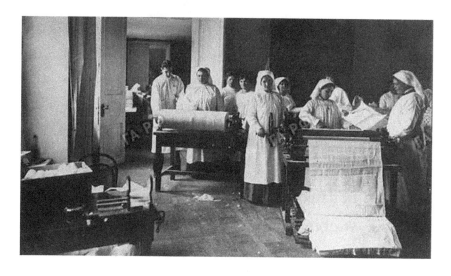

1914 letter from Olga to Nicholas II:

22 September. My dear golden Papa! Thank you very very much for your telegram which made us all happy. I am so happy that the darling is with you. And so nice about our victory. Thank God. All the wounded came alive, and the little flags on the maps were moved forward, i.e. to the West. We three are sitting in Mama's lilac [mauve] room and writing to you, while Mama is already in bed. She has a very bad headache. She regrets awfully that she cannot write to you. She kisses you affectionately and wishes you a good night. Nastasia and I walked a bit today and went to the warehouse[191]. There were about 6 ladies working [there], and Madame Sapozhnikova, [who is] incredibly

---

[191] Building where supplies for Tsarskoe Selo infirmaries were kept (see interior photo above)

fat, and most of the time [she] did everything wrong, so that Trina had to redo everything. At 6 o'clock Tatiana and I went to Anya's. Grigori and Zina were there, not Anya's but the one who comes to him often, very charming, and finally Princess Gedroitz. She decided not to give the lecture since Mama was not there, and [we] went to listen to Grigori. He poured tea for us and told us a lot of interesting things. He said that the strong rains helped us, and other good stuff. The weather is clear, but very cold—only 1 degree of warmth. "The Evening Flyer" [newspaper] just came. It says it came to the active army. Could that be true? A. I don't know why I wrote this letter ["A"]. Well, goodbye, sunny-Papa. Sleep well and dream of many good things. Forgive me for my silly letter. May God keep you. I love you very much and kiss you. I am with you with my entire soul. Always Your daughter

Elisavetgradetz.

Big regards [from] A.A.

1916 letter from Tatiana to Nicholas II:

23 September. Papa, my dear. I am sitting now in the morning before lessons, while Maria and Anastasia are playing the gramophone and raising the flag. Playing the March of the Escort Guard. After that, our hymn and some march which was played on the yacht. They brought a wounded officer to us, a Chernogoretz[192]. He was in the Kiev Corps for 7 years, and now is in 57th Maudlin Regiment. He does not know of course where his relatives are. He asks us, where King Nicholas and King Peter are, and where he is, we don't know and he is so anxious, since his

---

[192]Montenegrin

brother is Peter's adjutant. He is seriously wounded, poor chap. A huge wound on his back, his left arm is paralyzed, the right is wounded and the right hip. He is small and thin. I am glad that Nikolai Pavlovich is with you again. Today the grass is covered with frost and [there are] very few leaves [left]. Well, goodbye, Papa, my darling. I kiss you affectionately, and Alexei. May the Lord keep you both. Your much loving, Voznesenetz

From the 1917 diary of Nicholas II:

24th September. Sunday. After yesterday's incident

they did not allow us to go to church, fearing someone's resentment. Obednitza was at home. The day was superb: 11° in the shade with a warm breeze. Walked for a long time, played gorodki with Olga and sawed wood. In the evening read "Zapechatlenniy angel" aloud.

25th September. Monday. Lovely quiet weather: 14° in the shade. During our walk, the commandant — the dreadful commissar's assistant, ensign Nikolsky and three marksmen from the committee searched all over our house with the purpose of finding wine. Not finding anything, they stayed for a half hour and left. After tea they started to carry in our luggage which arrived from T. S.

26ᵗʰ September. Tuesday. Another magnificent cloudless day. In the morning walked a lot and read on the balcony before breakfast. Cut wood during the day and played gorodki. After tea unpacked the newly arrived rugs and decorated our rooms with them. Finished Leskov's novel "Nekuda."

From the 1913 diary of Olga Romanov:

Friday. **27 September.** Zlebov, Batushka and Kublitzky had breakfast, but my S. got sick at the last minute and did not come. Did not see him all day and [I] miss him. Played three sets with Papa against Rodionov and T. and won two sets. One was a tie, another—9:7. Then played 2 singles with T and won. Mama was there too. She has been feeling nauseous all day and has a stomachache. Had tea in the garden. Had dinner on the balcony. In the evening we 2 rode in a motor with Papa and Anya. Saw Grigori Yefimovich and N.P. in Yalta. Drove through the Lower Massandra[193]—moon, nice—13 degrees.

---

[193] The Massandra Palace had been built in the French chateau style by Count Vorontzov-Dashkov and acquired by Emperor Alexander III in 1889, who hired architect Maximilian Messmacher. The palace was finished in 1900. Prince Lev Galitzyn began the Massandra Winery in 1894, and the region was known for its delicious wines.

Dmitri Pavlovich to Nicholas II:

Paris, **1911. 28th September.** Dear Uncle,

Yesterday I received your charming telegram with your
wishes for my name day. It went to Petersburg, where
the office staff couldn't think of anything better but to
forward it to me by mail—via a registered letter.
Yesterday I sent a reply via a telegram, but thinking
that Aunt will of course be surprised by my late
thankfulness, I decided to write to you. It is strange
somehow for me to think that living in Livadia you

occupy a new, completely unknown house to me. I hope very much that it is to your taste.

How is "Alix's" health? May God grant it that the climate and the sun will benefit and help her. In Paris, "all is well." Papa is in a good mood, and his spouse too. Although neither one of them is completely healthy. The weather is lovely, although very cold—relatively speaking of course.

I will leave Paris around the 8th or the 12th of October and go directly to Petersburg, to the regiment, in order to start serving faithfully and truly. Most likely I will catch up with Maria and her husband, who will be here on the 8th or the 7th on their way to Siam. Time goes by quickly here, I go to the theater often. Saw a lot of funny plays and guffawed freely. Although I am tired of civilian clothes. Every morning one must think of shirts, stockings, suits and generally be involved in semi-lady like activities. I wish I could put on my dear uniform on soon. I am terribly sorry that I will not see your house in Livadia, and will not be dunking my white body into the sea waves like three years ago, and will not be playing dice with you, while teasing Zhylik and my opponent.

How are you, what are you doing? Ah, well, dear
uncle, I was thinking about you a lot during your
difficult visit to Kiev. I wanted to write, but thought
that you must have enough letters without me. I
imagine that this was not exactly of benefit to poor
Aunt. Well, now I embrace you firmly, and cover Aunt's
little hands with sweet passionate kisses, and ask her
not to forget her "son." Faithful to you with my whole
heart and soul, Dmitri

From the 1917 diary of Nicholas II:

29th September. Friday. The other day Botkin
received a document from Kerensky, from which we
found out that we are allowed to take walks outside of

town. To Botkin's question as to when this can start, the dreadful Pankratov replied that this is not even up for discussion right now due to some inexplicable concern for our safety. Everyone was extremely indignant by this answer. The weather got cooler. Finished "Ramuntcho."

194 Doctor Evgeni Botkin's pass into Governor's mansion.

Tatiana to Empress Alexandra:

30 September, 1914 – Tsarskoe Selo.

Mama darling mine,

Forgive me about the little dog[195]. To say the truth, when he asked should I like to have it if he gave it me, I at once said yes. You remember, I always wanted to have one, and only afterwards when we came home I thought that suddenly you might not like me having one. But I really was so pleased at the idea that I

---

[195] Dmitri Malama, Tatiana's favourite officer gave her a French bulldog puppy as a gift, which she named Ortipo, after Malama's horse. Ortipo went into exile with Tatiana and her family, and was killed along with them in July 1918.

forgot about everything. Please, darling angel, forgive me. Tell Papa about it. I hope he won't have anything against it. Good night, beloved Mama. God bless and keep you. 1000 kisses from your devoted daughter and loving,

Tatiana

Say, darling, you are not angry.

OCTOBER

From the 1913 diary of Olga Romanov:

Tuesday. **1 October.** Went to obednya. Mama also came but stayed in the chapel. Rodionov, Kublitzky, Zlebov, and Nevyarovsky had breakfast. Cold and very windy. Played tennis. Played 2 sets with Anya against N.P. and T., a tie. Then played "bumble" with Ippolit.

Papa played with Anya, T. and Rodionov. Mama was with N.P. After the game [we] went down to the beach to look at the surf. S. is in Kosmodemyansk, so what. However, it is awfully lonesome without him. [I] want to see him, as well as dear AKSHV. Had tea in Mama's purple sitting room. After dinner we 2 walked in Papa's jacket. 5 degrees.

196

From the 1917 diary of Nicholas II:

2 October, Monday. Warm day. About 4 o'clock it rained a little. Now all our people who wish to take a walk are forced to pass through the city escorted by the soldiers.

---

[196] View of the street from a second story window (possibly the grand duchesses') of Governor's mansion.

Dmitri Pavlovich to Nicholas II:

Petersburg. **1910**. **3rd October.** My dear Uncle, Forgive me that I have not written in so long, but I have very little time now, as the studies have already entered winter track. The last time I saw you and Aunt in Peterhof was on the 9th June, before your departure to the Baltic Port. At that time, I moved to Krasnoe and was enjoying it. I liked it an awful lot, service at the squadron interested me very much. Then I also had field trips with my tactics professor, colonel Belyaev. Here are also other things I wrote to you, Aunt Miechen (the rock of the family) was awfully nice to me. She was probably trying to prove that it could be really nice without you at Tsarskoe Selo, if I could only live with her for a bit, but she didn't succeed very well. I felt sad somehow, every time we rode by the Alexander Palace with Kirill or Aunt Miechen. Oh yes! It was so charming at Krasnoe, and I only just got a good taste of it and got used to the officers and lower ranks and was enjoying being with them at the big parade, when a telegram from Papa turned up, – that I had to immediately go to him in Bavaria. You can only imagine how happy I became! It turned out later that some nice people wrote to Papa that my health is getting ruined, that I practically have tuberculosis, – and of course Papa got frightened, but I was not touched by his fright at that moment at all! So reluctantly I had to leave Krasnoe, the wonderful weather that established itself there, and exchange all that for Bavaria, with its awful weather and almost as awful life. We lived in a hotel there, named Steinmetz Hotel, first class, but there was not a lot of first class there: the rooms were dark, damp, and my mood plummeted tremendously there. In addition to all that, the weather was devilish, beastly cold, and daily rain. Having spent five weeks in this paradise, I departed for Sweden. I must tell you of course that at the end of my stay at G[illegible], Aunt Marie arrived with her daughters and then it got better, as we rode in motors often, took walks and saw a lot of beautiful places, a lot more than if I just stayed at Papa's. He did not like to walk in the mountains, napped during the day, and read aloud in the evenings! It was wonderful at Maria's. I can honestly say that I did not expect this, as in the past years it was unremarkable, but I repeat that this time it was wonderful in Stenkmmar. The weather was delightful, I went hunting a lot. I was even invited to an elk hunt by the king; it was perfectly pleasant: although I did not kill anything, but there were a lot of elk. 11 of them were killed in two days. His majesty Le Roi was awfully congenial, and seeing that I was not terribly lucky, he put me under his own numbers (very very graciously). Besides that, we often went to balls from Stenkmmar, and in the evenings the people visited us, and in the end time went by so quickly and pleasantly, that the two weeks I stayed there went by like one day.

I returned to Petersburg on the 5th of September and started school almost right away. I do not go anywhere much, as no one is in Petersburg yet, only to the theaters. With great anticipation I am awaiting your arrival, in order to make "klops-shtos of yellow in the middle". Perhaps I will go to Moscow in late October, and by the way I wanted to speak with you about that. The thing is that my Fanagoryitzy are stationed in Moscow now. What shall I do? Most likely they will want to see me there. What do you order? Should I go see them this year or delay this visit until next year, under the guise of my coming into adulthood? Because if I go to them, I will have to do it officially. If you think I should delay my visit to the Fanagoryitzy until 1911, I can limit it to only receiving the regiment commander when I am in Moscow. Now I must end! Forgive me if I bored you with such a long message. Give Aunt my sincere love. May God let Friedberg benefit her. I hope so much that she returns to us very strong. I embrace you and the children.

Yours, Dmitri.

197

From the 1917 diary of Nicholas II:

4th October. Wednesday. Today we were reminiscing about the convoy holidays in the old times. It was warmer than it sometimes is in Crimea at the same time of the year. Good for Tobolsk! Spent the day as usual. After vsenoshnaya, Alexei got his gifts. Had dinner at 7 ½ o'cl.

---

197 Alexei is standing on the Governor's mansion balcony in this photo.

198

5th October. Thursday. Did not get to church for obednya on Alexei's name day due to the stubbornness of Mr. Pankratov, and at 11 o'cl. we had a moleben service [at the house][199]. In the morning it was foggy, wh.[ich] dissipated by one o'clock. Spent a long time outside in the fresh air. In the evening Alexei arranged cinematograph for us.

---

[198] A home chapel was set up in the large hall of the Governor's mansion after the imperial family was banned from going out to church for prayer services.
[199] See above.

From the 1913 diary of Olga Romanov:

Sunday. **6 October.** Went to obednya. Big breakfast as usual. Tennis in the afternoon. Lost 2 sets with Papa against Rodionov and T. N.P. sat with Mama. After that had tea at home. Tasha and Olga Kleinmichel were here before dinner. So lonesome without S. 10 degrees in the evening. Finally, it was warm the entire day. The fleet left at midnight last night. Mama is tired.

200

1915 letter from Maria to Nicholas II:

7 October. My Papa darling! I am writing out of turn, as Tatiana did not have a chance [to write] because of Petrograd. We, with Anastasia, deigned to visit the warehouse and roll the bandages, then went to our infirmary. A young officer from my regiment was supposed to arrive there, [he was] wounded in the leg in the 25th September attack. He said that lately the regiment has all been on horseback. He is really young, 18 and a half years old. He was presented to me on the 1st of June with two other officers, when he graduated from the Nikolaevsky Cavalier School. We only just consecrated the cemetery church with Mama,

---

[200] This is an actual photograph of the Brethren military cemetery chapel consecration, which took place on 5 October, 1915.

and already two officers died at our infirmary and the Grand Palace infirmary. I must end now as they came in to see if we have a letter for you. I love you very much and kiss you and Baby. + Kazanetz. Regards to Kolya.

From the 1913 diary of Olga Romanov:

Tuesday. **8 October.** Had a Russian language lesson at 11. Before that we 2 and Ira went to the beach to watch the high tide. Zlebov, Rodionov, Babitzyn and Nevyarovsky had breakfast. Played tennis. Played 1 set with A. against Papa and M. and then 3 more with Rodionov against Papa and N.P. We won 2 sets, and they won 1. Mama was lying down nearby. Did not see S., lonesome. Had tea at home since Uncle Sandro, Aunt Ksenia and Irina came over. Then— French reading. Mama went to Yalta to see Grigori

Yefimovich. After that she went to a glass store and bought a vase for each of us. Darling. She is terribly tired. [...] She did well. In the evening [I] helped Anya paste in the album.

From the 1916 diary of Maria Romanov:

9 October. Went to obednya. Ate a sample of the 1st Hundred's [food]. At breakfast sat with Ozerov and Maksimovich. Rode on the Bykov Highway, stopped near the chapel. Took a walk, saw two trains, the others boiled and fried potatoes. Had tea at Papa's. An Italian military agent came to the Marsengo train. [I] played the guitar and sang. Dinner 4 with Mama, Papa, Isa, Kiki and Anya. Played hide-and-seek, still [with] Mordvinov and Galushkin.

201

From the 1917 diary of Nicholas II:

10ᵗʰ October. Friday. The weather remained pleasant—around one degree of frost. Klavdia Mikhailovna Bitner, who arrived here two days ago, gave me the letter from Ksenia. Today she started to tutor the children, except Olga, in various subjects.

---

[201] Klavdia Bitner is on the right, in a nurse uniform.

From the 1913 diary of Olga Romanov:

Friday. **11 October.** We 2 had Russian lesson until 10 in the morning. Saw off the ship with the sailors who moved to the reserves. They waved their caps and yelled "hurrah" [when passed] by Livadia. We also waved, [it was] very sad. Papa left at 8 ½ in the morning to hike through Krasny Kamni to Ai-Petri and back, planned to return for tea. [We] had breakfast with Mama. She has a lot of pain in [her] lower back. Tennis in the afternoon. Played 2 sets with S. against T. and N.P. Then played with S. against T. and Anya. Then with Anya against S. and T., and, finally, with T. against S. and Anya. I played extremely badly and kept losing. Returned for tea with S., Anya and T. N.P. went to the Shirvansky regiment. Alexei has a pain in his leg and did not go outside. Worked in the evening. Papa read Averchenko's stories. 8 degrees.

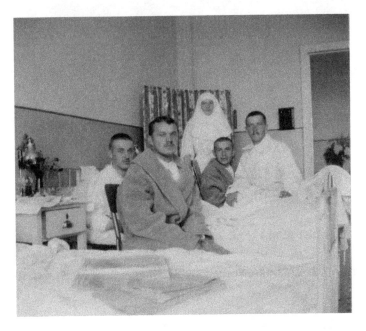

From the 1914 diary of Tatiana Romanov:

Sunday, **12 October.** Obednya in the morning. Prior to that I spoke on the telephone with Malama.[202] Breakfast 5 with Papa and Mama. In the afternoon walked with the sisters and Papa. Mama [rode] in a carriage. At 4 o'clock went to the Hussar infirmary to [see] the wounded. We 4 went to Anya's for tea. Shvedov and Viktor Erastovich were there. Anya

---

[202] Dmitri Yakovlevich Malama, a cavalry officer and love interest of Tatiana.

brought me a little French bulldog from Malama, incredibly sweet. So happy. Had dinner with Mama and Papa.

From the 1916 diary of Maria Romanov:

13 October. Wrote. Walked at Likhoslavl st.[ation]. Had breakfast with same as yesterday, and the same with dinner. Vikt. Er. came over, sat with us and smoked and drew. Everyone had tea. After the Tosno station, Vikt. Er. came over again and drew me, and of course I [drew] him, but mine came out badly. After dinner [we] arrived at Tsarskoe Selo. Went to the new and old infirmaries with A. Had tea 4 with Mama. Unpacked.

From the 1913 diary of Olga Romanov:

Monday. **14 October.** Had lessons. After that we 2 walked with Nastenka. Butakov, Kozhevnikov, Stolitza and Ippolit had breakfast. Tennis in the afternoon. Played 2 sets with Papa against T. and Rodionov, won 1 set each. Mama sat with N.P., her back still aches. Had tea at home with them. After dinner went to wish Alexei a good night as usual. He is better. At 9.15 in the evening we 2 went to a charity ball at Narodny Dom with Papa, Aunt Ksenia and Irina, benefit for the institution and temperance. Came back at about 11 at night. It was lots of fun. I danced 1 quadrille with Prince Trubetskoy. He was also the conductor. The 2nd dance, which was the cotillion, I danced with

Volodya Gantskau, the waltz—with N.P. and with dear Shurik, who was very jolly in his dark jacket. Saw my S. once—he passed in the quadrille. He seemed sad somehow, I don't know. There was a troika with ribbons. Shurik and another sailor [rode in it?]. When we returned [we] had tea with Mama.

From the 1915 diary of Tatiana Romanov:

Mogilev. **15 October.** Thursday. At 9 ½ in the morning [we] arrived here. Papa, Alexei, Dmitri and others met us. Went to the Governor's house, where they live. Sat there for a little bit, then while the Papa had a report, so we went to infirmaries with Mama. Went to 4. Breakfast with everyone at Papa's. Then went to the train. Papa came over to get us and we all went outside of the city on motors. I [rode] with M[aria], A[nastasia] and Dmitri. Walked a little. I was awfully happy to go with him. Had tea with everyone in our train. Then walked around the hospital train with Papa and Mama. At 7 ½ dinner at Papa's with everyone. Then sat with Alexei. Returned to the train with Papa and Dmitri at 10 ½. We sat at Dmitri's, and Papa with Mama together until 11 ½.

Dmitri Pavlovich to Nicholas II:

Petersburg, **1911. 16th October.** My dear uncle,

How happy I was to get your letter, you cannot even imagine. Even my valet noticed this, and having glanced at me with hungry eyes, asked: "Did anything happen?" Having read your letter, my soul felt so peaceful. Something dear and homey emanated from it, and for a minute I actually was speaking with you. After all, uncle, I have not seen you for a rather long time, and would very much like to. It has been three days since I returned from Paris, where time passed by wonderfully well. Only Papa was in a rather sour mood in the beginning of my visit, as he was not feeling well. Something intestinal! But then Papa became happy and pleasant again. As soon as I arrived in Petersburg, I ended up at the panikhida[203] for poor Strukov. Today I went to the regiment attire, we laid a wreath on the casket. Looks like we will not have to do the burial, as the entire Uhlan regiment is coming for that. (For this occasion, I think it would be nice if I dress in the Uhlan uniform—it was already ordered). All this I just mention by the way: it is all rather obvious and logical already. I feel sorry for Strukov. A nice and sympathetic person he was. Always so energetic and healthy looking. Your capitol, i.e. to be completely accurate—MY capitol, is not spoiling us with its weather. So sh..tty, that it's such horror. Muddy, cold. It is especially obvious

---

[203] Orthodox prayer for the dead.

after Paris, where it was 14 degrees in the mornings, and the sun blustered with all its strength.

Well, I now embrace firmly my illegitimate mother (my bad, I AM the illegitimate son, she is not the illegitimate mother). I give a wet kiss to the children. I pull you, not without some respect, into my embrace. Your faithful, with all my heart and soul, except of course for my ass,

Dmitri

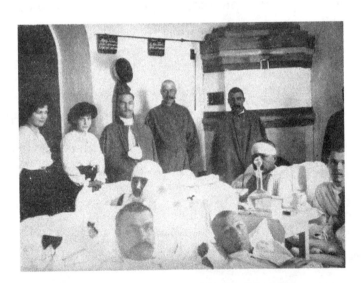

Letter from Anastasia to Nicholas II

17 October, 1916. Tsarskoe Selo. My golden Papa Darling! Just now I had arithmetic lesson and now I am free and have to write a lot and do homework. It's so nice that you are coming here! We are all awfully happy. There is snow on the ground today and it's kind of strange, but it is sunny, but 3 degrees below, the weather is so-so. Yesterday I got a very sweet letter from Mordvinov. Do you know if he sneezed when he got my letter from Orsha[204]. It is so pleasant to remember how nice and fun the time in Mogilev was, and how we used to play hide-and-seek in the evenings. When we were returning it was very nice that Viktor Erastovich was there, otherwise it would have been terribly boring, and he sat with us for a little while in the afternoon and after dinner. It was cozy! Now we have lessons, we go to the infirmaries and all is the same there. We do not have any new wounded at our infirmary, only an officer from Maria's regiment, a Kazanetz. Mama is going to her infirmary for dressing changes in the mornings for now. Yesterday afternoon we rode with Mama, Anya and all four of us. Did not run into too many people, almost no one was out walking. Yesterday Mama received Countess Karlova and her daughter Merica, as she is planning to get married in November, so she returned, [she is] rather cute. Maria just passed by here and sends you a big kiss. I think she now has a history lesson. Well, my Papa Darling it's time for me to end.

---

[204] Anastasia was known for pranks, this may have been one of them.

I send you and Alexei an awfully big kiss 1000 times. Regards to Mordvinov. May God keep you. Your loving loyal and faithful little 15-year-old Kaspiyitz.

From the 1913 diary of Olga Romanov:

Friday. **18 October.** Had lessons. At 11 in the morning we 2, Nastenka and Ira went shopping in Yalta. Batushka[205], Schepotiev, Rodionov and Kozhevnikov had breakfast. Tennis in the afternoon. Overcast, chilly. Won 1 set with A. against M. and Shanpersky. Lost 2 sets with N.P. against Shanpersky and T, then played 1 set with Papa against T and Rodionov. Mama was there and after 6 in the evening [she] went to a

---

[205] Orthodox priest

chapel in Yalta. Zborovsky was there too. Had tea as usual. Shurik was not invited. Such a shame. S. left for Bakhchisarai and Simferopol, so [I] did not see him. After dinner sat with Mama. Papa read the report from torpedo boats. Windy. 8 degrees. Washed [our] hair.

From the 1914 diary of Tatiana Romanov:

Sunday, **19 October.** In the morning everyone went to obednya. Had breakfast 5 with Papa and Mama. Had tea and lunch with them. Sat at home with Marie and the doggie. At 4 o'clock we 4 with Mama, Anya went to our infirmary. Sat with the sharpshooters for a while, then on the 3rd ward, Karangozov, Mikhalevsky and Iedigarov. The Uhlans are in the city. Went to Anya's. Nikolai Pavlovich was there. Went to vsenoshnaya at the Lower church. Talked on the telephone with Karangozov and Iedigarov.

From the 1916 diary of Maria Romanov:

20 October. Went to Petrograd with Papa, Mama, O. and T. to the Fortress, for the funeral obednya for Grandpapa.[206] Had breakfast 5 with Papa, Mama and Igor.[207] Walked 4 with Papa and Mama [rode] in an equipage[208]. Had tea and went to vsenoshnaya, the same confessed. Had dinner 4 with Papa, Mama and Igor.

---

[206] Emperor Alexander III.
[207] Prince Igor Konstantinovich, son of Grand Duke Konstantin Konstantinovich.
[208] Carriage.

Dmitri Pavlovich to Nicholas II:

Petersburg, **1910. 21st October.** Dear Uncle,

I was awfully, awfully grateful to you for your dear letter. I was so terribly happy to get it that I honored it by standing up. And the entire time I read it, I was respectfully standing, bent in half.

I am awfully happy that you are coming here, as I want to see you so terribly much. Here in Petersburg there are rumors that there will be court balls this year, and I hope this is not true! And if it's true, then I already see myself in a waltz vortex with Zizishka

Naryshkina. What a lovely couple!

Winter is in full swing here, freeze and a lot of snow, and the merry Petersburgers are riding in their sleighs already. Poor things, they think that winter is here already, but it's not! Soon it will be warm, and the streets will be [covered in] cloaca!

I visualize the hat, which my sister pulled onto her pedigreed head, about two meters in diameter. Such beauty!

Lessons have started at school, but they are significantly easier than last year. Again, one can hear from the maneges: "Forward, strokes—left hand arrive." How familiar those sounds are to me, how much they speak to one's heart!

Lots of new officers at the courses, and the most charming of new recruits—is your Petrovksy cuirassier. An awfully important feeling overcomes me at the thought that I am no longer a new recruit, but a senior one.

The officers are saying that their tails fell off, those who were at new recruit courses, and now there is only a scab, and they call the new ones tailed beasts!

Once again, I thank you for the letter. I laughed a lot from yours, although from respect I used the letter E: hehehehe and not hahahaha!

I respectfully kiss the hand of her majesty.

Yours, Dmitri

From the 1916 diary of Tatiana Romanov:

Saturday, **22 October**. In the morning [we] two went with Mama to Znamenie, from there—to the infirmary. Took photographs in two stages in the sitting room, since last time the pictures did not come out. Later dressings for Syroboyarsky, Bogdanov. The others— Mama. Also took photographs in three other wards. In between sat with Volodya in the hallway. Later played bloshki[209] with Volodya, Petrov and Lieutenant Girs. Later the lieutenant had gone and was replaced by— Prince Eristov. Then said goodbye to Volodya. It was so sad, he and seven more are going to the Crimea today, Bogdanov, Vinogradov, Galakhov, Pavlov, Jurgenson, Kamensky, Motsidarsky. Breakfast with Papa, Mama and Gavriil[210]. Walked in the afternoon. Mama—in a small equipage [carriage]. Read. Had tea with Papa and Mama. Went to vsenoshnaya. Met up with Yuzik's brother. Had dinner with the same [people] as breakfast. After went to say goodbye to Alexei and little Makarov, Zhenya and Lyolya. They came to visit Alexei yesterday. Spent the night with us and were together all day, and will spend another night again today. Sat at Mama's downstairs. Worked. Anya was here. Then Papa came.

---

[209] Tiddlywinks.
[210] Prince Gavriil Konstantinovich, second son of Grand Duke Konstantin Konstantinovich.

From the 1913 diary of Olga Romanov:

Wednesday. **23 October.** Had the first painting lesson with N.P. Krasnov. At 8 in the morning Papa went hunting in Kosmodemyansk and returned after 6 in the evening. Had breakfast with Mama and Prince Trubetskoy[211]. He feels well after surgery. In the afternoon we 4 went to Lower Massandra with Mama, Anya, Ira and Nastenka. Finally saw my S. with Kublitsky and Ippolit in the rose alley. Played different games: the sorcerer, cat-and-mouse and oskar. It was not that much fun for me. Was very happy to see S. Mama sat, walked, picked flowers. [We] stopped at a

---

[211] Prince Nikolai Sergeyevich Trubetskoy, a Russian linguist and historian at court.

meadow where Alexei was. They had tea, baked potatoes in charcoal and rolled around in hay. After dinner Papa read Teffi to us. Raining. 10 degrees. Helped Anya paste in the album. Mama read. She is tired. Shame that Shurik wasn't there.

From the 1914 diary of Tatiana Romanov:

Friday, **24 October.** Lesson in the morning. Stopped by the church for a minute. From there to the infirmary. ... Later stood in the hallway with Iedigarov, a little with Ellis and others. Today Mama's 5 Crimeans, one other, and little Ellis are leaving for the Crimea. It was terribly sad to part from them.

Breakfast [we] 5 with Mama. At 1.30 we two went with Mama to Petrograd. I had a meeting from 2:15 to 3:45 in the Winter [palace]. Then Isa and I went to Holy Cross community, where we met with Mama and Olga. Returned at 5.30. Had a lesson. Princess was here. Had dinner 4 with Mama.

1914 letter from Maria to Nicholas II:

25 October. My dear Papa darling! I am terribly sorry that I did not have time to write to you. This morning [I had] the obnoxious lessons, as always. Then [we] had breakfast. In the afternoon we went to 4 infirmaries in Pavlovsk with Mama and Aunt Mavra, and saw a Cossack who was wounded by a Saxon swine (i.e. their equerry). I am writing so badly, because [I am using] Mama's quill. Just now I washed up, and Liza[212] is combing my hair. Also, today we went to the consecration of Svodny Regiment's infirmary. It is located in the building where the church used to be. A dining room was set up in that room, and there moleben was held right there. Where we used to leave our coats is now a room for dressings. Demenkov, my darling, of course was not there. After vsenoshnaya tonight we went to the infirmary, where Iedigarov was [admitted]. I kiss you affectionately, my golden one. Your devoted and loving Kazanetz. Big regards from me to Sasha and Kolya. Grigori was just here. He will remain in Petrograd until you get back. God be with you. +

---

[212] Maid to the grand duchesses

Dmitri Pavlovich to Nicholas II:

Petersburg, **1911**. **26ᵗʰ October.** My dear Uncle,

You are probably totally not expecting the reason for which I picked up the quill to write you this letter. And actually, the business for which I decided to bother you is so incredible that it is even strange for me to write about it.

The thing, uncle, is that I beg of you to allow me to go to the war theater between Italy and Turkey.

A long time ago now, from the start of the war action, I

wanted to approach you with this request, but thinking that the war will soon be over, and that it will have a character more like a military expedition than a real war, I was hesitant to write to you. But, it seems that the war is inflaming, and a quick resolution cannot be expected.

This is probably the only chance, my dear uncle, which will let me to see war, from the side stage so to speak. As you yourself know, I went through almost the entire academic course for tactics, strategy, fortification and administration, and it would be wonderfully educational to compare theory with practice. From the Italian side, all the latest military news is applied. Aeroplanes for example, have already served big! I would want terribly, if it is possible of course, to go there on the side of the Italians: since we did have some foreign princes on our side in the Russo-Japanese war. I would like to learn more, closer and familiarize myself practically with military business, and I repeat, I doubt this type of opportunity will arise again. Work at the manege, training of young soldiers and horses— is interesting, but understandably one cannot compare it all with such an experience as war.

Already in Paris I spoke with Papa about this that I want to ask your permission to head to Italy, and he has no objections—from his part. The regimental superiors will let me go too. Uncle, I beg you, think about my request and perhaps you will allow me to fulfill my wish. I kiss you affectionately, "my mamasha" and the children. Your faithful with all my heart, Dmitri

1914 letter from Tatiana to Nicholas II:

27 October. Papa dear darling. We are sitting at Mama's after lunch. Anastasia has gone to bed, Marie is still sewing, she sits on the floor and works, while Olga [is] in Your chair. Mama is speaking on the telephone with Sonia. You know, Merika Karlova is marrying an Orzhevsky Horse Guard. I do not remember what he looks like. Yesterday evening from 6 until 7.45, we sat at our infirmary. Alexei was there too. Many officers were not there, as they went visiting, while we sat with the ensign of your Nizhny Novgorod regiment, who told us a great deal about the war. He had just been involved in the business that day outside of Skernivits, where they so distinguished themselves, and he showed us the bullet hole in his sword, and its end has a trace of blood of the Skernivitsy (as they say), where he himself chopped up many [of them]. Such a shame that you did not see them and that they could not tell you all of this—so interesting. He, that is this ensign, was in the Bulgarian war, took Adrianople with them and got their [St] George Cross from Ferdinand himself. Now he is embarrassed to wear it, and he hides it. It is so lonesome, darling Papa, because You are not here, it is terrible. Today I received some kind of Archimandrite, who at the same time is the senior doctor at my infirmary in Minsk. Unfortunately, you were not there, and so he told me that the soldiers cried terribly. Then he told me that [one of] his patients is your Commander of the Shirvan Regiment, Colonel, I think Trotsky, I do not quite remember the last name. Well, now, good-bye, my sweetheart, God bless You. Your very loving daughter Voznesenetz. Regards to Nikolai Pavlovich and Drenteln. If you see Sashka to him too.

From the 1916 diary of Olga Romanov:

Friday. **28th October.** We 4 with Mama had breakfast on the train on the way to the city. T. and I went to her committee, after which I received O. B. Stolypina.[213] The Little Ones[214] went around the infirmary at the Grand Palace with Mama. There are currently 358 people there. Tea on the train with Viktor Erastovich. It's drizzling and awfully dark, but

---

[213] Widow of Prime Minister Pyotr Stolypin, who was assassinated in a theater in Kiev in front of Nicholas, Olga, and Tatiana.
[214] Maria, Anastasia, and Alexei.

warm. Now Mama is receiving. Papa telegraphed from Kiev. They went to Grandma's for her fiftieth wedding anniversary. In the evening we 4—to the infirmary. Played the piano in the sitting room. Mitya came in toward the end. Returned after 11 o'clock. Rain.

1914 letter from Maria to Nicholas II:

29 October. My golden Papa! This morning, we have lessons, as always. Alexei has time to write to you today, as he will not have a lesson with Pyotr Vasilyevich. Yesterday evening at half past ten Mama went to the train. Before that Malama was here, he was very sweet. Today all snow melted and the weather is very spring-like, only the grass is not green. Right now, it is drizzling a bit. The sisters rode with Anya, Olya and Resin. In the afternoon, Anastasia and

I will probably go to our infirmary. We have this one soldier there who does not say anything, but is awfully sweet. For some reason he loves bracelets and played with one of mine for a long time. We have three soldiers who cannot write at all. One of them learned to read a little with us. We have four officers. One is tall, [he] stinks and is afraid of dressings, and has a wife. Another is fat and not too smart. The third, a regiment commander, always has a bunch of visitors, and the fourth is leaving today it seems. Nikolaev just arrived here from the Svodny Regiment, [he] was wounded, and we are going there now. I kiss you very affectionately and love you. Your Kazanetz. May God keep you. +

From the 1913 diary of Olga Romanov:

Wednesday. **30 October.** Had lessons. Zlebov, Babitzyn, Kublitzky and Smirnov had breakfast. Tennis in the afternoon. Lost a set with N.P. against Rodionov and T, then played 2 sets with Papa against them and tied. Zborovsky and Shaprinsky also came over. Shame that Shurik wasn't there. By now I am used to S. not being here. Mama also came. Cold but not windy. 7 degrees in the afternoon. 5 ½ degrees in the evening. Moon. Had tea as usual. In the evening played Kolorito with Mama. Papa read in his [room].

From the 1914 diary of Tatiana Romanov:

Friday, **31 October**. Lesson in the morning. Went to Znamenie. Rode to the infirmary to [see] ours. ... Later sat in the hallway with all the officers. Went to the Big House for a single operation, come back to our [infirmary], and took photographs of a lot of them. Breakfast and tea at home. During the day sat at home too. At 5:30 we said goodbye to Alexei and the sisters and rode to the train. Had dinner with Isa, Anya and Resin.

NOVEMBER

1915 letter from Anastasia to Nicholas II:

1 November. My sweet and dear Papa Darling! It is very lonesome here without you. We just went to vsenoshnaya and already had dinner with Mama. The snow melted already but the Gale is blowing with all its strength, and this is not very pleasant. Well, I am starting a new day. In the morning we went to obednya as usual. Skorikov, Paleny and Kalashnikov were there. Today is the holy day of Kozma and Damian. We rode in the afternoon, then [we] went to the sisters' Palace infirmary. There was a concert they played the balalaikas, the Tolstoys and many other acquaintances, it turned out very nice. We returned just now. It was raining, but 4 degrees of warmth and very slippery. I can imagine very well how you have dinner and breakfast and imagine all your companions. I am writing to you and Alexei at the same time. I am hurrying because I now have to do my boring homework. "Go to sleep, achievement of fame, all go to sleep!!!" Olga is resting now, while Maria is winding up the gramophone, this is pleasant. All three sisters smooch you a lot, and I do too of course. 100000 big kisses, your loving loyal and faithful Kaspiyitz. Sleep well +.

From the 1917 diary of Nicholas II:

2nd November. Thursday. During the night it abruptly froze up, in the morning [it was] down to 11°. The day was sunny with a northern wind. Took a walk as usual; during the day hauled firewood. In the evening Olga received some modest gifts.

From the 1895 diary of Nicholas II.

3 November, 1895: "A day I will remember forever . . . at exactly 9 o'clock a baby's cry was heard and we all breathed a sigh of relief! With prayer we named the daughter sent to us by God 'Olga'!"

From the 1914 diary of Tatiana Romanov:

Tuesday, **4 November.** Had a lesson. Drove to Znamenie, then to our infirmary with Mama. During Kusov's surgery, we sat on the third ward and talked a lot. Then changed dressings .... Then we went to a surgery at the Grand p.[alace], returned to our [infirmary] and stayed with the officers in the hallway for a little while. Breakfast and lunch with Papa, Mama and Count Sheremetiev. Had a lesson. In the afternoon walked with Papa and Mama [rode] in a charabanc. Had tea upstairs. The Princess was here, and we took the final surgery exam. Had a lesson. After lunch, went to Olga's meeting. Saw Grigori at Mama's.

Note from Empress Alexandra to Tatiana:

5 November, 1916. My dear, Anya asked me to come to the laying of the foundation of the church at 12:30 (Our Friend[215] will be there). Can at least one of you four come with me, otherwise I will be completely alone, as I do not have even one lady in waiting?

Mama +

---

[215] Grigori Yefimovich Rasputin.

From the 1913 diary of Olga Romanov:

Wednesday. **6 November.** I am upstairs with Alexei. Had lessons. Then had breakfast downstairs with the hussars, Butakov, Zlebov, Kozhevnikov and Babitzyn. Tennis in the afternoon. I stayed home, had a healing mud application on my leg. Had had tea with everyone: N.P., Butakov, Shurik, Zborovsky. Dinner was downstairs at 7 in the evening. Masses of people. Mama came later, greeted everyone, and the ball started. T. and Anya opened it. I danced a quadrille with the warrant officer Delinkov, a cotillion—with Prince Trubetskoy. Towards the end [I] waltzed with S. for a while. He danced with the Kleinmichels the entire time. The threesome was there: Shurik, Zborovsky and Ippolit. [It was] rather nice and merry. About 40 couples. [It] ended at 1 in the morning. 7 degrees.

From the 1913 diary of Maria Romanov:

7 November Thursday. In the morning 4 with Papa toured the ship "Peter the Great" and stopped by the yacht. At breakfast sat with Uncle

tennis 4 with Papa; Mama, Anya, Kiki, Pi, Shurik and Zborovsky were there. Had tea at home. Read in Russian. Had dinner with Anastasia.

From the 1913 diary of Tatiana Romanov:

8 November. Sunday. [...] Sat with Mama. Had tea all together. Then had lessons. Went to dinner in Kharax[216] with Papa and Olga. The same as last time [we] were there. Then took a walk. Returned at 11 ¾.

---

[216] English-style palace in the Crimea, home to Grand Duke Georgiy Mikhailovich. It was named after the largest Roman military settlement excavated in the region.

From the 1913 diary of Olga Romanov:

Saturday. **9 November.** Sat on the balcony for a ¾ of an hour in the sun. Mama did not sleep well, she is tired and her back aches. N.P., Zlebov, Batushka, Stolitza and 4 artillery officers had breakfast. The 1st brigade holiday. Tennis in the afternoon. I did not play. S., Shurik and Zborovsky were there. N.P. sat with Mama. I am cold. [Not as cold as?] yesterday, but still not warm. At tea [I] sat with S. and Shurik. Had dinner downstairs with the Emir of Bukhara. He is leaving tomorrow. Mama was also there. Went to vsenoshnaya. 6.5 degrees. Went to bed at 11 o'clock.

From the 1917 diary of Nicholas II:

November, Friday. Another warm day—it went to zero. During the day I sawed wood. Finished the first volume of "1793." In the evening I read Turgenev's "Memoirs of a Hunter" aloud.

11/24 November, Saturday. Much snow has fallen. No newspapers or telegrams have come from Petrograd for a long time. At such a grave time this is serious. The girls were occupied with the swings, jumping from them into a pile of snow. At 9 o'clock there was vsenoshnaya[217].

---

[217] Vespers service

1915 letter from Tatiana to Nicholas II:

12 November. Papa darling. Yesterday I was in town, had a [committee] meeting at the Winter Palace. [It] was so tiring. Maria was also with me. Since it was her first time at my meeting, Neydgart decided to give her a few words of welcome. So, he and the others all got up and bowed to her. She almost crawled under the table in horror. Then we had tea at Grandmama's. Uncle Sandro was there and the three boys, who of course were naughty and did not obey. It must have been nice to see the Nizhnegorodtzy, huh? The other day we went walking with Trina –Maria and I, and Mama allowed us to leave the garden, and we walked almost to Pavlovsk Park. Poor Trina was pretty tired because I forgot and walked too fast. Mama is still not feeling particularly well, and does not go to the infirmary. Papa darling, it is so lonesome here without you. Well, goodbye. May God bless you. I kiss you and the little one firmly and gently. Your Voznesenetz.

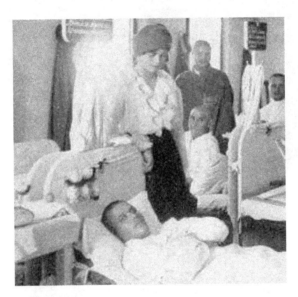

Letter from Maria to Nicholas II:

13 November, 1915. My dear Sweet Papa! Heartfelt wishes for Grandmama's birthday and the wedding anniversary. We had tea at Grandmama's, and I think will go see her again tomorrow. She is very happy with her trip to Kiev and told us that she visited some infirmary every day. Right now [we] will go riding with Nastenka. Then Anastasia and I will go to our infirmary. Yesterday they brought 7 lower ranks there

from the train. Rather seriously wounded, we have not
seen them yet. Anastasia is sitting next to me, reading
something. I have not seen Nik. Dm. It is rather
boring for 2 weeks already. Since they had put a
couch in the sisters' bedroom, it became much cozier, I
kiss you and Alexei affectionately. Your Kazanetz.
Regards to all. Our arithmetic teacher is healthy again
and is coming to [teach] us again.

From the 1917 diary of Nicholas II:

14/27 November, Tuesday. Birthday of dear Mother
and 23rd anniversary of our wedding. At 12, there
was a religious service. The choir got things mixed up

and sang out of tune, probably because it had not been rehearsing. The weather was sunny and warm, with gusty winds. After afternoon tea, I re-read my earlier diaries—pleasant occupation.

From the 1913 diary of Olga Romanov:

Friday. **15 November.** Had lessons, after that [we] went shopping for wool with Nastenka as usual. It rained in the morning, [was] wet. No sun in the afternoon. S., Rodionov, Zlebov and Shepotiev had breakfast. Papa received Mongolian ambassadors extraordinaire. Walked through the farm beside and behind Mama's carriage, Mon Jardin and Livadia. N.P., Rodionov and S. came along [with us]. I walked with darling S., [it was] so nice. Had tea all together. We 2, Papa and Mama went to Kharax for dinner. The same [people] were there and did the same things. Uncle Georgi – no, Uncle Mitya – yes. Returned at 11 o'cl 20 min. 5 ½ degrees.

1915 letter from Tatiana to Nicholas II:

16 November. Papa darling dear. I rejoice so much that we will see each other the day after tomorrow, it is so nice. The weather here today is disgusting, overcast and cold, but yesterday was wonderfully sunny. The other day we were at Grandmama's for obednya, then had a family breakfast in the Blue

Room, and then in the afternoon had tea at Anya's and two of our wounded were invited. Yerevanetz Shakh-Bagov and Your sharp shooter from the 3rd Regiment Kiknadze, and also the huge Rita Khitrovo was there. Our time there was very nice and cozy. Mama was at Uncle Pavel's at that time, and then she stopped by for a moment. Pyotr Vasilievich came over now before the lesson and is playing with Ortipo. He was terribly pleased to receive a letter from Alexei. Do you walk during the day or do anything else? Well, good-bye, Papa darling. May God bless you. I kiss You and Alexei firmly. Regards to Nikolai Pavlovich and Dmitri. Your Voznesenetz.

Dmitri Pavlovich to Nicholas II:

St. Petersburg, **1911. 17th November.** Dear Uncle, I thank you terribly for your charming letter and for treating my request so positively. Of course, it would be even more pleasant for me if I got an affirmative response to my request, but for a no—there is no trial. So I will try to work here too. I will try to do my best to give feasible assistance to our common goal! We are starting to get new recruits now, although there are no classes for them yet. They are still only looking around and moving through the barracks uncertainly and with major civilian appearance. I often read in the newspapers about what you are doing in Livadia. And I admit that every time I feel sorry that I am not with you. How are the evening dances? It would have been a perfect opportunity for me to grab Zizishka's hips and run with her, or for example to squeeze Baroness Fredericks with sweet passion and dance with her, forgetting everything around us! He! He! He! There are no evenings in Petersburg yet, thank God, and I hope there won't be for a long time yet. I hate those fashionable evenings. You enter, stunned, everyone seems like a stranger. Kiss the hands of young ladies, do not look at the married ladies. Ah! It is horrible, and then the visits the next day. Devil may take them! The weather is nice here. Two, three degrees of frost, clear skies, sunny, but no snow, although personally I think that it will soon appear (snow). I am hearing rumors that my mamasha (Alix!) is not behaving herself. Meaning in terms of her health. This is not good. Tell her that I am very unhappy about this. Let her remember me or the poor postal worker, and maybe then she will feel better. Well then, I embrace you firmly. I seek sweetly and passionately the same with my lips with Aunt, and cover the children with juicy but chaste kisses (let them wipe themselves).

Yours Dmitri

Dmitri Pavlovich to Nicholas II:

Paris, **1913. 18th November** st.st. Dear Uncle,

It will probably seem strange to you that I am suddenly writing to you, but having read my whole letter until the end, you will see what this is about. My holiday ends in two weeks, but most likely I will leave for Petersburg before this time, specifically around the 23rd and 24th of November.

I came here in order to live peacefully, but it turned out somewhat differently. This whole sad story with my sister upset and disturbed us all very much, it was all so fast, and, I will even say—unexpected.

I would rather not speak about it too much in a letter, and you know almost everything already from the letters that were sent to you, and also if I am not mistaken from the words of Sazonov, who was in the Crimea.

I was supposed to leave Paris two weeks earlier, but thought it prudent to wait in Paris until Papa found out anything about Maria's business. And now everything we wanted to know—we know, and I am moving on to the question which prompted me to bother you in this letter. Would you allow me to come to you in the Crimea for about one—two weeks, upon my return to Petersburg. It would be so nice for me to see you, and I would love to speak to you terribly much. You always listen to me so charmingly and nicely.

If my arrival at Livadia is a possibility, then I can be there around the 6th-10th of December.

If you would be so kind as to respond to my letter with a telegram or a letter, then write directly to Petersburg.

My time in Paris passed rather quickly, but still I wanted to be back in Russia. What's difficult here is that there is not much to do. Of course, after serving at the regiment it is nice to spend 3-4 weeks like a leisurely gentleman, but then the regiment is calling to me again and my work. I go out a lot here. Society is charming to me, and I get a lot of invitations.

I found some nice horses here and ride almost every morning. I don't do any neck-breaking things and will tell you straight up—I am longing again for my horses, to jump.

The weather is wondrous. Some are completely summery days. Sunny and so warm that it is too hot to walk in a coat.

Well now, forgive me for bothering you. I firmly kiss her majesty's little hands and smooch the children touchingly. Faithful with all my heart and soul

Dmitri

I thought about you a lot when I found out about Dedulin's death. Memory eternal for him!

1914 Letter from Maria to Nicholas II:

19 November. My darling Papa! Today I am the one writing to you, as Olga and Tatiana just went to Petrograd for the charities. I had lessons in the morning. Mama rode in the train with Olga, Alexei and Anastasia. Yesterday I was at the Grand Palace with Mama and the sisters, to see the wounded officers and saw that young officer who had a big bed sore on his back. He has a very sweet face. We signed his cards, and now he is waiting for you to return and maybe sign for him too. Right now, it is two o'clock. Mama is lying on the couch and writing you a letter, while Anastasia—to Aunt Olga. At 2.30 Anastasia and I will go to our infirmary. Probably new [patients] also arrived there. At tea I always sit in your chair. Mama got a letter from you before breakfast. Later she will go to the Grand Palace for dressings of two officers. Alexei is upstairs resting after breakfast. Tomorrow Chakhov is going back to the front. I am so happy that it's a holiday on Friday, so that we will not have lessons, and this is very pleasant. Today during the arithmetic lesson, the teacher bent down to see if I wrote something correctly, and broke the chair leg with his weight, and almost fell on me. Well so long, goodbye my Darling. I kiss you affectionately and love you. Your Kazanetz. May God keep you + Regards to Sasha and Kolya and tell the latter to behave.

218

From the 1917 diary of Nicholas II:

20 November/December 3, Monday. The frost increased and the day was clear. There was disaffection among the soldiers because they had not received their pay from Petrograd for three months. This was quickly settled by a temporary loan of the necessary sum from the bank. During the day I busied myself with the firewood. At 9, there was a vesper service.

21 November/December 4, Tuesday. This day of the

---

218 A. Kirpichnikov, yard keeper at the Governor's mansion in charge of firewood.

Feast of the Presentation we had to go without church service because Pankratov[219] did not deign to permit it. The weather was warm. Everybody worked in the yard.

From the 1913 diary of Olga Romanov:

Friday. **22 November.** Had lessons and went shopping in Yalta with Nastenka. S., N.P., Zlebov and Stolitza had breakfast. I was so happy to see him, but also had a heavy heart for some reason. Foolish. Tennis in the afternoon. Won 2 sets with Sumarokov against Papa and Anya. Then won 2 sets with A.

---

[219] V. S. Pankratov was a Commissar sent from the Capital.

against Sh. and M. and won 1 set with Sh. against A. and Zborovsky. Rodionov was there. N.P. sat with Mama. Had tea with them as usual, as well as dinner.

From the 1913 diary of Maria Romanov:

23 November, Thursday. Had lessons in the morning. At breakfast sat with Uncle Nikolasha and Count Shtekelberg. In the afternoon 4 played tennis, Papa, Mama, Anya, Kiki, Kolya, Shurik, Zborovsky and Sumarkov were there. Had tea at home. Went 4 with Papa to vsenoshnaya. At dinner sat with Komorov and Nilov.

From the 1913 diary of Olga Romanov:

Sunday. **24 November.** Obednya at 11 and a big breakfast. Afterwards Mama came downstairs. [It] drizzled a little. We 4 went to the Lower Massandra with Papa and Mama. Mama brought her carriage, and we walked along the Rose Alley with N.P. and Rodionov. A little after 4 o'cl. [we] went to the yacht. Stayed there. It was awfully nice. At about 5 o'cl. [we] went to the saloon and 23had tea there with the remaining officers. [It was] so cozy, but [it was] such a shame that S. was not there. The crew returned from the cinematograph accompanied by music. At 6 o'cl.

Mama, Anya and I went to the Red Cross Sanatorium. It was very nice. All [patients] there have tuberculosis. Returned at 7 o'cl. Ran into Sh. at the waterfront. Stopped by Trina's. In the evening sat with Mama. 6 or 7 degrees.

1914 letter from Tatiana to Nicholas II:

25 November. The Alexander Palace. My darling Papa, how are you doing? Is it nice for You in the Caucasus? I want so much to be with You. Yesterday Sashka had tea with us, as he is going to the Caucasus, I think, and Iedigarov had dinner with us. Today we have to do the dressings and two surgeries. Aunt Ella came over to have breakfast with us today, and tomorrow she will be at the panikhida at 5:30 at the Palace infirmary church for the dead officers and the lower ranks of your Nizhny Novgorod regiment, and on the 27th on their regimental holiday there will be a moleben. This they asked for, and we will be there with Mama. Ortipo is terribly sweet and was with me again in Vilna and Kovno. And there she had her first walk. Is Nikolai Pavlovich happy to be with You? Did you get the "Invalid" which I sent You with the letter? We were terribly sad that we did not find Nikolai Nikolaevich in Kovno with the others, as they were sent on an expedition. We saw Voronov in Vilna. We were traveling in a military motorcar, and they in a carriage. Your Yerevantzy came over to see us, lieutenant colonel Matchavariani, lieutenant Kazumbekov and Lieutenant Tikhonov. Well, good-bye, my dear Papa. Send my regards to Nikolai Pavlovich and Drenteln. Your Voznesenetz embraces you firmly and loves You fondly.

From the 1917 diary of Nicholas II:

26th November. Sunday. Today is Georgievsky holiday[220]. The town arranged a dinner for the Calvary and other entertainments in the People's House. There were a few Georg. Cavaliers But in the ranks of our guards whom their non-Calvary comrades decided not to relieve, and forced them to serve – even on such a day! Liberty!!! Walked a lot and for a long time, the weather was mild.

---

[220] Holiday honoring those decorated with the St. George Cross.

From the 1913 diary of Maria Romanov:

27 November Wednesday. In the morning went to Yalta and had lessons. At breakfast sat with Nilov and Count Apraksin. In the afternoon 4 played tennis, Papa, Mama, Anya, Kiki, Kolya, Shurik, Zborovsky, and Sumarkov were there. Had tea at home. Read in French and Russian. Had dinner with Anastasia and Alexei.

From the 1913 diary of Olga Romanov:

Thursday. **28 November.** Walked to Yalta with Nastenka. 35 m. [It was] damp and muddy. N.P., Kozhevnikov, Schepotiev, Nevyarovsky had breakfast. Papa and Mama rode in the afternoon since Papa's leg still hurts. We 4 went to Oreanda on the horizontal trail and down with Anya, N.P. and Kozhevnikov. When we returned [we] played hide-and-seek in the dark with Sh. and Kozhevnikov. It was lots of fun. The rest of them played kosti upstairs. Had tea all together. Everyone from Kharax and Kichkin had dinner. After that we wrote. Mama is tired. Alexei is sleeping. 8 degrees.

Letter from Anastasia to Nicholas II:

29 November, 1915. Tsarskoe Selo. My dear Papa Darling! We just had breakfast with Lolo Dolgorukaya and I ran from there in order to write to you. Nothing much happened except that we went to Anya's yesterday and Viktor Erastovich and Nikolai Dmitrievich were there. This was after dinner at 9 o'cl. Well that was nice. And this morning we went to obednya and ran into Viktor Erastovich. He said that Shvedov arrived here. Before obednya Gulyga came over to bid farewell to Mama, he is leaving today too. Well that is all the news, and the rest is the same as usual. Right now, it is snowing hard and is 10 degrees below. Yesterday Maria Pavlovna the Younger had tea with us and looked very adorable because she has curly hair, they curled it for her and it looks very good on her, so we approved. Yesterday during our ride, we ran into Countess Paley[221], alone in Pavlovsk on skis, it was so cute, she could hardly move her legs. When we rode past her, we hooted with laughter a lot and for a long time, but of course she did not see or hear us. Tell Alexei that "Joy" sends kisses and misses him a lot. He came to us this morning and sat near us and was so sweet but sad. Does the door from your study to the white hall creak? Regrettably I must end. I feel sorry that this letter is so boring, but we never do or see anything interesting, but continue putting on "Vova Has Adapted" and sing the same things we did when you were here. I send you and Alexei a big kiss and squeeze you in my modest embraces. Your loving loyal and faithful Kaspiyitz.

---

[221] Second—and morganatic—wife of Grand Duke Pavel Alexandrovich

1914 letter from Maria to Nicholas II:

30 November. My golden Papa! Mama is now lying on the couch and resting. This morning all of us, 5 with Mama went to obednya and then to change dressings, and Alexei also watched and counted how many he was present at. After breakfast we took [photographs] with the wounded officers at the Grand Palace. From there we went to the Invalid House[222], and there Mama gave out St George's medals to several lower ranks. Mama is very tired, and therefore

---

[222] Sort of a nursing home for disabled soldiers

she will not write to you today. We will now have tea with Uncle Pavel. Yesterday at vsenoshnaya I saw my darling Demenkov, while Shvedov was at the meeting. So both Olga and I were very happy. Yesterday afternoon we went to the local infirmary, where Mama also awarded medals. Today after tea Mama will receive the officers, her two Crimeans, one from my regiment and the other from Olga's. I kiss you affectionately, your always loving Kazanetz. May God keep you. + Regards to Kolya and Sasha.

DECEMBER

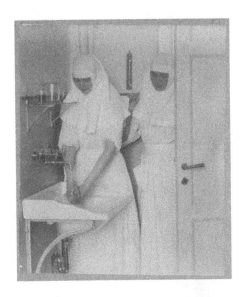

1915 letter from Tatiana to Nicholas II:

1 December. My dear Papa. Thank you for the greetings that we received from You through Prince Chavchavadze and Navruzov. They told us how nice it was, and said that when You promoted them to the next rank, they had the feeling as if they graduated from school. They were as happy as they were back then. They both had tea and we had a very cozy time. They told us about one little captain who distinguished himself in the Caucasus at Sarakamyshin. Extremely interesting. Everyone tells You a lot of interesting things, huh? Is it true that all were promoted except the Guard? They told us so. Papa darling, send them our regards when you see them. Yesterday evening we were at Anya's. Viktor Erastovich was there, Alexander Konstantinovich and Ravtopulo, who accidentally ended up here a few days. How is Alexei? Tell him that Joy is bored without him. Ortipo is terribly sweet. Well, good-bye, my darling Papa. May God bless You. I embrace you dears. Your Voznesenetz.

From the 1913 diary of Olga Romanov:

Monday. **2 December.** At 9.15 in the morning, we 2 and Papa went to Ai-Danil for a children's sanatorium consecration by the sea and on the border with Gurzuf. Returned at about 11:45. Rodionov, Batushka, Smirnov and Nevyarovsky had breakfast. After that Grigori Yefimofich's wife Praskovya and Varya[223] went to Mama's, [they] sat together for a while. At 3 ½ N.P. arrived, played kosti with Papa, Mama and Anya as usual. S., Rodionov, Sh. and Zborovsky first went downstairs to see Alexei, then [we] played hide-and-seek. Sh. and M. were searching the entire time and could not find everyone—it was

---

[223] Varvara Rasputina, daughter of Grigori Rasputin.

time for tea. S. is so sweet, and Sh. is also nice. It was fun. We 2 and Papa had dinner in Kharax. Then played the same games. All is well. Returned at 11 o'cl. 20 min. 5 degrees. Rain. Alexei is sleeping.

Dmitri Pavlovich to Nicholas II:

Petersburg. **1909. 3rd December.** Dear Uncle,

Allow me to bring you most heartfelt congratulations for the 6th. Such a shame that you are not at Tsarskoe, I could have congratulated you in person.

Time flies by awfully fast in Petersburg, nevertheless winter cannot pass without a death—[we] buried George of Mecklenburg. He will never tell me "May God keep you, darling" at the exit again.

I have a lot of homework, the entire day is stuffed with it, what else is there to say, but that the studies at the dear military school—are just pure joy. The officers in the courses are adorable; there are of course bad ones among them, but very few.

Soon is the school's anniversary, and I wanted to ask your permission, when I see you, to allow me to partake in the celebrations as an officer in the course there.

If this is possible, it would be very pleasant for me.

Life in Petersburg is much more peaceful this year, and I am speaking of the entire venerable family of Countess Gogenfelzen, we see each other very rarely, and in any case, I am not suffering because of that.

And now, in order not to remind you of Aunt, who loves to write tomes, allow me to bow out. Heartfelt regards to her majesty.

Yours, Dmitri.

From the 1916 diary of Maria Romanov:

4 December. Went to obednya 5 with Papa and Mama and the same had breakfast with Toto. Showed Toto our rooms. Walked 5 with Papa. Saw off Papa and Alexei (they went to Mogilev). Went 4 to a concert at the G.P. Had tea 4 with Mama and Anya. Went to the old infirmary with A., played checkers. Stopped by Nastenka's and Isa's. Had dinner 4 with Mama, the same went to the sisters' infirmary. Played checkers with Shareiko.

Tatiana to Grand Duchess Olga Alexandrovna:

5 December, 1915. [...] Poor Sonia was buried today. Mitya and Vera Orbeliani have just arrived, poor things. There were a lot of people. It happened all of a sudden and she was taken too awfully soon—in only two days. Mama was with her the entire time. She was almost unconscious, and could not even speak or open her eyes. However, every time Mama called on her, she blinked her eyes, letting us know that she could still hear but could not speak. Her aunts were here too, and came over to her every hour. Her face had changed and turned so yellow. The priest gave her last rites, and while she was slowly getting nearer her end, he gently read the prayer for the dying. She was buried here at the Kazan cemetery. I had just one lesson today. Everything is working well at the infirmary [...]

From the 1917 diary of Nicholas II:

6th December. Wednesday. Spent my name day quietly and not like in the previous years. At 12 o'cl. a moleben service. The marksmen of the 4th regiment in the garden, former guards, all congratulated me, and I them—with the regiment holiday. Received three name day pies and sent one of them to the guards. In the evening Maria, Alexei and M. Gilliard acted in a very friendly little play "Le fluide de John;" there was a lot of laughter.

7th December. Thursday. The freeze came down to 22° with a strong wind, which cut the face, nevertheless we successfully went outside in the morning and evening. In my study, in the daughters' room and the hall it is very cold—10°, which is why I wear my Plastun cherkesska all day until nighttime. Finished part II of "World History."

From the 1913 diary of Maria Romanov:

8 December Sunday. In the morning 4 with Papa went to obednya. At breakfast sat with Dmitri and Count Shtekelberg. In the afternoon 4 played at home, Mama, Papa, Dmitri, Anya, Kiki, Kolya, Shurik and Zborovsky were there. Had tea at home. At dinner sat with Dmitri and Count Shtekelberg.

From the 1917 diary of Nicholas II:

9th December. Tuesday. Got a nice letter from Olga [Alexandrovna]. It got colder, it was windy and clear. After my walk I tutored Alexei. Finally, after intense heating it got really warm in the rooms.

From the 1913 diary of Olga Romanov:

Tuesday. **10 December.** Last visit to the dentist with Shura. Stopped by the pier. Saw N.P. and my S. on duty. N.P., Kublitzky, Stolitza and Batushka had breakfast. In the afternoon we 3, Papa and Dmitri walked on the horizontal trail, hiked up the Cross Hill and the rocks. Very fun. Smoked. Wonderful weather. 7 degrees. The terrible storm at night tore down the cypress trees near Papa's window. M. stayed with Mama. Anya left. Had dinner at a quarter to 8, and in 1 hour we 2 went to Narodny Dom with Papa and Dmitri to see the play "A Life for the Tsar." It was fantastic. N.P., Sh. and S. were there, but I felt sad for some reason. Mama was still up. 5 degrees. Returned at 11:45.

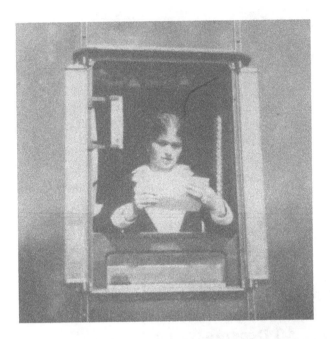

From the 1916 diary of Olga Romanov:

Sunday. **11th December.** On the train between Novgorod and M[illegible] across the r[iver] Kerest. Departed tonight at 3:10 and arrived in Novgorod at 9 ½ in the morning. At 10 went to Sofiysky Cathedral. There was an Arkhireisky service and moleben until 12, paid respects to various holy relics. Downstairs stopped by the storeroom with ancient artifacts and got home by 1 o'clock. At 2 o'clock, went to Zemskaya Hospital, and my female mon.[astery—i.e. nunnery] . . . kissed the icons, etc. . . . then to the orphanage for the refugee children, and Yurevsky male monast.[ery], [located] 5 versts from the city. Drank tea at the table with the nobles. From there to the chapel, where Our Lord's Mother appeared in sorrow, and remained. Terribly nice and such a wonderful smell in the chapel. Was able to fall asleep before Tsarskoe, where we arrived at 12 hrs 20 min. at night.

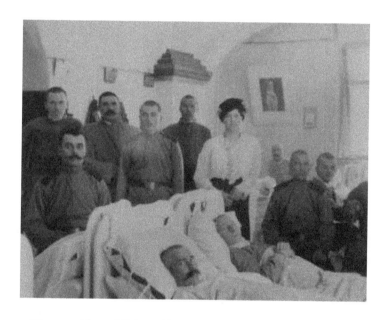

From the 1916 diary of Maria Romanov:

12 December. Arrived at Tsarskoe Selo. Went to the old and new infirmaries with A. Had breakfast and tea 4 with Mama. Rode in a troika with Isa. Sat and read. There was music. Had dinner 4 with Mama and Grigori at Anya's. Went to the infirmary 4 with the sisters. Played ruble, then checkers with Shareiko.

From the 1914 diary of Tatiana Romanov:

Saturday, **13 December.** Tsarskoe Selo. At 11 o'clock arrived here. Breakfast, tea and lunch with Mama. Alexei is upstairs, Marie has angina. In the afternoon 3 with Anya went on a sleigh ride. Rode to the Great Palace to the wounded. Went to vsenoshnaya. Saw Shvedov. At 8.30—went to our infirmary with Anya. Was very glad to see everyone. Many new ones. Anya got terribly sweet letters from Malama and Iedigarov. Papa sent a telegram from Novoborisov.

From the 1913 diary of Olga Romanov:

Saturday. **14 December.** We 2 and Nastenka went shopping in Yalta. While we were at Zembinsky's S. walked by. [It is] warm in the sun. Zlebov, Stolitza, Batushka and S. had breakfast. Finally, my real [code: "loved one"], although [I] think I said 1½ words later, but still. May the Lord keep him. In the afternoon [we] walked through the settlement and the farm—muddy and swampy. N.P., Zborovsky and Kozhevnikov. Poor Sh. is still in bed, he is running a fever. Had tea as usual. Went to Kichkin and Kharax for dinner and vsenoshnaya. [We] played the piano. 4 degrees in the evening. Alexei rode to Massandra.

Letter from Anastasia to Nicholas II:

15 December, **1916.** Tsarskoe Selo. My Dear Papa Darling! You already know well about our trip to Novgorod as I think Olga wrote you a lot about it. In my opinion it went very well! It was so cozy to sleep in the train and the feeling was a little like we were going to see you in Mogilev. Maria just came over and is sending you a big kiss. Well Christmas is so soon! We are all waiting for you! This Tuesday I was remembering and imagining how you were going to the theater. Right this minute I got a letter from Zhylik and the continuation of the "Mysterious Hand." I have not yet read it so we will read it aloud all together, more interesting that way! I think that today Igor is leaving you, on 15 December? We just had breakfast with Kozhevnikov, who arrived in Petrograd a few days ago, but soon he is leaving again. He told us masses of interesting things—how their transfer went and etc. He remains the same. Well now, Papa my Darling it's time for me to end. May Christ be with you. I send you and little Alexei an awfully big kiss. Your loving loyal and faithful little 15-year-old Kaspiyitz.

From the 1913 diary of Tatiana Romanov:

"The Standart." **16 December**. Monday. In the morning went to the orphanage for the chronically [ill] with Nastenka and Olga. I feel terribly sorry for all of them. Returned at 11 something. At 12 there was a molebna. Had breakfast with everyone. [...] Later Papa bid farewell to the troops in front of the house and ceremonial marshals passed by. At 3 o'cl. 40 min. we 4, Papa, Mama, Alexei and Dmitri rode to the yacht in two carriages. We 4 [rode] with N.P. Had obednya on the deck. Stayed with P.A. for a little while, then went to tea. After tea we 4 with Mama and N.P. went [back] to the yacht, got in a motor boat and went to the chapel of Nikolai the Miracle Worker near the mall. Prayed and returned to the yacht. Walked around the yacht with the officers. Had dinner with everyone. Later [I] was with P.A. for a little while, then Olga sat with him and N.P. until 11 ½. It was awfully nice. Went to bed at 11 ½."

From the 1913 diary of Olga Romanov:

"Alma[224]. 10:06. Tuesday. **17 December**. Sailed out to sea at 5 in the morning. The yacht rocked a little, nice. Arrived in Sevastopol at 8.35 and docked. Salutations. I was in the control room with S., Rodionov and Kublitzky. At 10 in the morning Papa went to dedicate something at the aviation school. We were there too until breakfast at 12 ½. In the afternoon Mama was lying down on the quarter deck. Very warm and a warm wind. Her heart is 2 ½. In the afternoon [we] took lots of pictures on the deck. Then sat in control room with my [in code: "beloved"] S., he

---

[224] Crimean River

wrote in the log journal, and we stayed there. He does not feel well—headache and cough. It is so nice to be with him. Papa returned after 4 o'cl. Had tea with all the officers at 5 o'cl. Then went to look at the train with N.P., S., Rodionov and Ippolit. I sat on the deck, but S. did not come. Extremely sad. A molebna was held on the deck at 7:40. After that the officers and the crew lined up on the wharf, we bid our farewells and left. [It was] terribly hard. 13 degrees. The yacht illuminated our way with searchlights. Went to bed at 10 o'cl. Mama is already in bed. May the Lord save everyone and S."

From the 1913 diary of Maria Romanov:

18 December Wednesday. In the morning read with Trina. At breakfast sat with Papa and Ivanov. In the afternoon 4 sat at Mama's. Had tea 4 with Papa, Dmitri and the suite. Read with Trina. At dinner sat with Papa and Dmitri.

From the 1916 diary of Olga Romanov:

Monday. **19th December.** As usual, to Znamenie and to the infirmary. Almost nothing to do. Went with Kasyanov to the drawing room and behind closed doors, without anyone present, I played and he sang various new beautiful things. Ate with Mama. Found out for certain that Father Grigori was murdered, most likely by Dmitri and thrown from a bridge by Khrestovky. They found him in the water. It's so terrible, should not even write. Sat and drank tea with Lili and Anya and the entire time felt Father Grigori with us... at 6 o'clock met Papa and Alexei. Such joy. Had dinner together. After 10 o'clock Papa and Mama received Kalinin, then Uncle Pavel. We were in Anya's rooms. At 12 o'clock to bed.

From the 1913 diary of Tatiana Romanov:

20 December. Friday. Unpacked the entire morning. At 12 o'cl. tried on dresses, the dressmaker was here. Had breakfast at 1 o'cl., all five with Papa, Mama and Count Grabbe. In the afternoon walked to Znamenie with Papa. Mama rode there with Alexei. From there took a walk. Walked to the park. Had tea downstairs with Mama and Papa. Papa left for dinner at Grandmama's in Piter. We three had dinner with Mama, Anya and Isa. Then Isa left and we two stayed with Mama and Anya until 10 ½. So lonesome with our [friends], being so far away.

From the 1916 diary of Maria Romanov:

21 December. Went to Grigori's funeral 4 with Papa and Mama and others. He was buried at Anya's construction. Had lessons, history and Batushka. Had breakfast 4 with Papa and Mama. Went to the old infirmary with A. Walked with Papa. Went to the new infirmary with A, and Vikt. Er. was there. Had tea 4 with Papa and Mama near Alexei, he has worms in his belly. There was music. Went to Anya's, saw Matryona[225], Varya and Akulina. Had dinner 4 with Papa, Mama and Sandro. Anya was here. Papa read.

---

[225] Maria Rasputina, daughter of Grigori Rasputin.

From the 1916 diary of Nicholas II:

22 December. Thursday. Sandro was here to see me in the morning. At 12 ½ went to the itinerant church in honor of Anastasia's name day. Mordvinov had breakfast and dinner. Walked with him and the daughters around the park. At 4 o'cl received Protopopov, and after tea—Pokrovsky. Studied in the evening.

From the 1913 diary of Olga Romanov:

Monday. **23 December.** At 10 o'clock we 2 and Anya went to see her niece Tatiana, T.'s goddaughter. After that, walked in the garden with Trina, M., and A. Very cold, 13 or 14 degrees below. Mordvinov had breakfast. In the afternoon [we] decorated the [Christmas] tree. Had tea and dinner with Mama and Papa. Helped Mama with the gifts until 7 pm. She is awfully tired, got almost no rest, in addition Lili Obolenskaya came to see her. Went to bed at 11. At 6 o'cl. the beaming and happy S. came over to Anya's. Thank you, Lord. 9 degrees.

Dmitri Pavlovich to Nicholas II:

24 December, 1914. Petrograd. Uncle, my dear, I want to write a couple of words to you. First, I send you best wishes for the holiday and the coming new year. May God give you all kinds of happiness. I wanted to show up by you, and even asked when I can arrive, but then it turned out to be impossible, and yesterday I was at my father's where I found out that you are ill. If your health allows me to come over at some point to Tsarskoe, I would be very happy. The thing is that I would really like to see you and Aunt before my departure to Moscow. I have the approximate departure date on 26th December. But, if it would be convenient for you to summons me on that day or the next—I can easily postpone my departure for two-three days. My health is fair, but cannot say that it is completely satisfactory. The doctors are laying big hopes on my stay in Moscow, or more exactly in "Usov." They are exiling me there for about six weeks, after which I hope to be completely healthy and return to service. Well, with this I embrace you tightly. Sincerely and deeply faithful to you

Dmitri

From the 1915 diary of Tatiana Romanov:

Friday, **25 December.** In the morning everyone went to church. Mitya and Volodya were there. Was very glad to see them. Breakfast with Papa and Mama. At 2 o'clock went to the Manège for a Christmas party of the Convoy Composite Regiment and took turns giving out gifts. Had tea all together. At 6 o'clock [we] 5 went to our infirmary for a party. Gave gifts to everyone. Then all sat in the drawing room. At first with Mitya for a bit. Then with Volodya. Was terribly pleased. Talked cozily. Returned for dinner. Anya was there. Read in the evening. Papa is [wearing] [his] Yerevan uniform.

From the 1917 diary of Nicholas II:

26th December. Tuesday. The same kind of quiet frosty day—13°. Everyone slept a lot. In the morning stopped by the guard room with the children—the 1st platoon of the 1st regiment was there; yesterday we sent them a tree, a sweet pie and a checkers game. The other day Isa Buxhoeveden arrived, but was not allowed to see us on Pankratov's caprice.

From the 1916 diary of Nicholas II:

27 December. Tuesday. In the morning had reports—from Shuvaev and Bulygin. After breakfast went to the riding hall for the third and last Christmas party. The Railroad regiment choir played beautifully again. Took a walk with Tatiana and Maria. The weather was excellent, sunny and frosty—8 deg [...]. After tea [we] had cinematograph—the same theme as in Mogilev. Alexei's right arm started to hurt from a bruise; poor thing, he suffered a lot at night. Studied for a long time after dinner.

From the 1916 diary of Maria Romanov:

28 December. Went to the old infirmary with A. The Metropolitan came over to praise Christ. Had breakfast 4 with Papa and Mama, Anya and Groten. Went 4 to the G.P. Walked 4 with Papa. Went to a concert at the new infirmary with T. and A.

Plevitskaya was there and Vaganova danced. Had tea
4 with Papa and Mama, dinner with same. Anya was
here, pasted in the album with her and Shvybz—
Alexei was in bed all day, his arm hurts and [he] slept
badly.

From the 1913 diary of Tatiana Romanov:

29 December. Sunday. Went to the regimental
church in the morning. Had breakfast with everyone.
[Went] to the train at 2 o'cl. 7 min. and we four went to
Grandmama's in Petersburg with Nastenka. Aunt
Olga was there. We sat there until 3 o'cl. 10 min. then
went with Aunt to her [place]. She changed clothes
and we went into the sitting room. Shurik, Yuzik, Vik.

Er., Vasily Vasilievich Sklyarov and Vyacheslav Vasilievich Beliy came over. We sat and chatted, played. Then we had tea. Marie Claire, Irina, Felix[226], Andrusha, Feodor, Sasha with his brother and mama, all came over. Then we 4, Shvedov, Yuzik, Georg. Gr. and Sklyarov played the charades on the stage. It was awfully nice and fun. Then we played various other games. After tea [we] went into the sitting room. Played "the whip" [...] Had dinner all together, at our table sat: Aunt Olga, Marie Claire, Yuzik, Beliy, Marie, Georg. Gr., Anastasia, Sklyarov, Olga. The rest sat at another table. After dinner we talked for a little while, then at 8 o'cl. 35 min. [we] went home. Sat with Mama and Papa and worked until 10 ½. It was extremely fun and awfully nice. [It was] P.A.'s birthday.

---

[226] Prince Felix Yusupov, fiancé of Princess Irina Alexandrovna

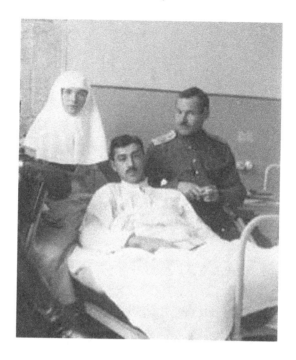

1915 letter from Olga to Nicholas II:

Wednesday. **30th December.** Mitya had a physical, later he came back and almost the entire time we sat together, played checkers and did just plain nothing. He is so good, Lord knows. Grandmama had breakfast. At 2 o'clock saw darling Papa off with Mama. So sad. From there to Znamenie. At 3 o'clock to a Christmas party at the House of Invalids. Later we 2 rode around in a troika with Isa. Had dinner with Mama in the playroom. In the evening talked with Mitya. Unexpectedly he received instructions to go to the Caucasus for about two days. So sad. Early to bed, have a head cold.

From the 1917 diary of Nicholas II:

December 31/January 13, Sunday. Not a cold day, with a gusty wind. Toward evening, Alexei got up. He was able to put on his boot. After tea we separated, till the arrival of the New Year. Lord, save Russia.

CPSIA information can be obtained
at www.ICGtesting.com
Printed in the USA
FSHW011957010919
61655FS

9 781537 683096